SWIMMING AGAINST THE TIDE

Swimming against the Tide

FEMINIST DISSENT ON THE ISSUE OF ABORTION

EDITED BY

Angela Kennedy

OPEN AIR

This book was typeset by
Woodcote Typesetters in
11 on 12.5 point Ehrhardt for
OPEN AIR
An imprint of FOUR COURTS PRESS LTD
55 Prussia Street, Dublin 7, Ireland
E-mail:fcp@indigo.ie

A catalogue record for this book
is available from the British Library.

ISBN 1-85182-267-4

Printed in Ireland
by Colour Books Ltd, Dublin

Foreword

PROFESSOR MARY MC ALEESE
Pro-Vice Chancellor, Queen's University, Belfast

There is an infamous passage in St Paul's letter to the Corinthians, which says, 'Women are to be silent in Church. They are not permitted to speak.'

As with so many people who have been colonised in one way or another the strength of the coloniser lay in silencing the colonised. Their voices, including the voices of women, have been relegated to whispers from the margins. In my lifetime the whispers have first grown stronger and then emerged as strident full volume voices insisting on their intrinsic moral, human right to speak and be heard without seeking permission. The aural space now occupied by the authentic and courageous voice of women keeps growing exponentially but there is a sad irony about the current phase of our evolution towards full social, cultural, economic, political and spiritual equality. That irony stems from the fact that new voices are telling women they do not have permission to speak and those voices are often the very voices which insisted most successfully and relentlessly on the need and the right to break the silence. Nowhere is this more evident than in the debate on abortion where pro-choice feminist agenda settlers have colonised the space, planted their flat and proclaimed that henceforth where the gospel of feminism is preached it shall be preached their way and no other way. Others may come who call themselves feminist but these will be bogus because when their credentials are checked they will be missing the pro-choice badge of admission. The myth that to be feminist is to be pro-choice has forced many women to resign from the name of feminism, to settle back bruised into the silence of the margins, victims of a new colonisation of the intellect. Why feminism should appear to be so uncomfortable with diversity and even conflict within itself on this issue is probably due more to its relative immaturity as a political and social force than anything more formidable. Still, there is a growing impatience with its failure to deal with the issue and move on. We are all getting much too long in the tooth to be told by the self-styled elder stateswomen of the sisterhood that we 'are not permitted to speak'.

This book speaks out of that impatience. In the pages which follow feminist voices challenge from inside the recent received wisdom that to be a feminist is naturally to be pro-choice. There is nothing natural about the deliberate and widescale lawful and routine elimination of babies. When those babies are all girls as in some cultures the right to choose lobbyists must surely begin to feel a distinct wobble in their gut. Wrongheaded arguments lead to wrongheaded outcomes. Is there a willingness to countenance the possibility that there is something missing at the core of the pro-choice argument, that maybe it is time to pen up the debate to a wider audience, new voices? These voices are not all the voices of the enemy. So often the abortion row has masked the commonality of purpose between its feminist proponents and its feminist opponents. True, both sides have had some unseemly and cringe-making allies, whether fundamentalist bigots or anarchic antimasculinists, but there is plenty of space in this new and growing territory of freedom of speech.

Things happen in closed worlds where vulnerable people suffer in silence and there is no one or no thing sufficiently powerful or sufficiently credible to vindicate their pain and their voice. A lot of bad things happen because those closed worlds are perfect environments for exploiters who thrive on the weakness of others and who are adept at creating plausible, hermetically sealed masks to hide behind. The louder the voices from inside those worlds the smaller the hiding place for the exploiter. There is a day coming when we will hear the voice from inside the womb, when its own authentic pain will be undeniable, when we will know with certainty that it is saying, 'I want to live. I have a right to live. I do not need your permission to live.'

Contents

FOREWORD — v

PREFACE — viii

INTRODUCTION: A FEMINIST CRITIQUE OF ABORTION — 1
Angela Kennedy

A LOST SOURCE OF STRENGTH AND POWER:
THE LONG FEMINIST TRADITION OF NON-VIOLENT
RESPONSE TO CRISIS PREGNANCY — 12
Mary Krane Derr

EMPTY RHETORIC: A FEMINIST ENQUIRY INTO ABORTION
ADVOCACY AND THE 'CHOICE' ETHIC — 28
Breda O'Brien

ABORTION, ECONOMICS AND WOMEN'S SEXUALITY — 38
Diana E. Forrest

SOCIALISM AND ABORTION — 46
Ann Farmer

THE NATURE OF THE FOETUS: A VEGETARIAN ARGUMENT
AGAINST ABORTION — 57
Ali Browning

ABORTION AND DISABILITY: IS THAT DIFFERENT? — 67
Marie-Claire Darke

IS ABORTION GOOD FOR WOMEN? — 75
Rachel MacNair

ALTERNATIVES TO ABORTION AND HARD CASES — 86
Patricia Casey

OBSTINATE QUESTIONINGS: AN EXPERIENCE OF ABORTION — 96
Catherine Spencer

CONCLUSION — 109
Angela Kennedy

NOTES ON CONTRIBUTORS — 116

INDEX — 119

Preface

The editor and contributors would like to acknowledge, with grateful thanks, the following people, whose help, information, support, advice, comments and encouragement have helped us to write this book: Sylvia Ayling; Sue Beresford and Margaret Killengray of the Insitute for Contemporary Christianity; Shelley Bovey; Dr Margaret Brierley of the Institute of Jewish Affairs; Paul Callaghan; John Carmody; the Catholic Housing Aid Society; CHAR (the Housing Campaign for Single People); the Child Poverty Action Group; Pauline Connor; Brendan Conroy; Paul Darke; Alison Davis; Margaret Denny; Lesley Dove; the Equal Opportunities Commission; Alan Farmer; Feminists for Life of America; Katharine A. Gilchrist; staff at Hale End Library, Highams Park, London; Alison Hartley; Barbara Hollinghurst; Felicity Jaffrey; Lois Keith; the late Jim Kennedy; Steve Stephanie and Sean Kennedy; Mary Kenny; Phillipa Linklater; Lion Publishing Company; Rita Lomax; Tony Lucas of the Movement for Christian Democracy; Sara Maitland; the staff of the Library at Middlesex University, Enfield; Linda Naranjo-Heubl; Bob O'Donnell; Mary O'Rawe; Rosemarie Rowley; the teaching staff of the M.A. Gender and Society programme at Middlesex University; staff at the Library of Royal College of Nursing, London; Damien Sarsfield; Shelter (the organisation for homeless people); the late Brendan Shorthall; Elaine Storkey; Agneta Sutton; Boyd Tonkin; Harriet Wade; Debby and Paul Wakeham; Paul Williams; and not least our publishers at Open Air.

The editor particularly wishes to thank her friend, colleague and fellow contributor, Ann Farmer, for her help and wise counsel in bringing this project to term.

Introduction:
A Feminist Critique of Abortion

ANGELA KENNEDY

We, the contributors to this book, are presenting a feminist critical analysis of abortion. This should seem a perfectly legitimate undertaking. 'Pro-life' feminists, like those termed black feminist, or socialist feminist, or lesbian feminist, are fragmented identities providing what Sandra Harding would describe as a 'rich source of feminist thought'.[1] Yet Germaine Greer tells us, 'For a feminist to express the opinion that being "for" abortion would make about as much sense as being "for" amputation is to jeopardize her feminist credentials.'[2] This telling statement says much about the litmus test that is applied to any woman daring to call herself a feminist. If she expresses any reservations with the 'party line' that abortion is a 'right', something women need and want, she is censured, censored and often summarily excommunicated from the movement by others who have similarly designated themselves as feminists.

Feminism, as a movement, has run into some problems. The first British 'national' women's conference at Ruskin College, Oxford in 1970 may have united over four 'demands' – equal pay, equal education and opportunity, abortion on demand and 24-hour nurseries. But as Nyta Mann has observed, 'For women at large, even uniting around the first demands . . . is difficult . . . women who would happily endorse all the demands determinedly avoid the label "feminist".'[3]

In these 'post-feminist' times, women are supposed to have achieved equality and fair treatment. Everything is supposed to be going well for us. Yet the strangled cry, 'I'm not a feminist, *but* . . .' is still heard. Women may still feel victims of injustice, and may place this injustice within a context of gender. But why is feminism now such an unpopular word? There have been a number of reasons advanced. Some feminists have blamed the decrease in feminism's popularity on a 'backlash' movement perpetrated by men who fear feminism's power, or believe it is due to a resurgence of conservative values in the eighties, the rise of the 'New Right'.[4] Others have criticised certain aspects of the feminist movement, such as the campaigns against date rape[5] or pornography, even the personalities of prominent 'feminists',[6] as not being relevant to women's needs today.

Although this book criticizes abortion and inevitably some pro-choice feminists will be criticized within its pages, we are not criticizing feminism *per se*.

There may be disagreement as to why women are oppressed (or even if they are oppressed), but the search for justice and equality for women remains a reasonable and necessary aim, however discomfiting the F-word is to some people. Yet, it is also quite possible that some of the unpopularity of feminism can be attributed to the alienation of 'ordinary' women who feel feminism has failed to take into account their dissenting views, on abortion, work inside the home, the family, or the idea of 24-hour nurseries, for example. There has, unfortunately, been an arrogant contempt for women whose views do not toe the 'feminist' line.

Many women who oppose abortion have been cast away from the fold of feminism, labelled anti-feminists.[7] Others themselves reject the women's movement, initially because of abortion, but then come to believe that feminists are not really interested in women's needs at all. Still others keep their reservations to themselves, fearing the predictable response a voiced criticism of abortion will bring. Many pro-life women have agonized over whether they have any right to call themselves feminists, and some pro-choice feminists have decided they have not,[8] including such a doyenne of feminism as Gloria Steinem.[9]

This despotism has undermined feminism. If the aim of feminism is to provide justice for all women then all women's voices need to be heard, even if they do not fit conveniently into pigeonhole responses. Marginalizing pro-life women out of feminism silences women's voices in the same way that they were silenced by patriarchy. Such wrongs have not been lost on anti-feminists, who assert that feminism places women's rights above human rights, that feminism does not reach 'real' women.[10]

The silencing of pro-life women is particularly ironic when other lines of dissent and differences flourish within the feminist movement. Jane Fonda perpetuates a beauty philosophy that could very well be said to undermine women, yet is called a feminist. She even writes publicity blurbs for Gloria Steinem books![11] Camille Paglia declares herself a commonsense feminist, even while she pours scorn on women who attempt to combine motherhood and intellectual fulfillment, and, despite her protests to the contrary, appears to believe we are after all, biologically determined —men, as rampant sex machines, and pregnant women as slow-witted.[12] Some feminists oppose pornography, but opposing views by anti-censorship feminists are always aired. Alix Kates Shulman has noted, 'Feminism is not a monolith; there are many different, even at times contradictory, positions which may spring from good feminist motives.'[13] Hester Eisenstein, like Shulman, acknowledges the internal splits and debates in a large political and social movement and how that movement needs to sustain those divisions. And she also believes, 'It is of great importance to be clear about what some of the differences are.'[14] Robin Rowlands acknowledges, 'It may be that [feminists] . . . are underestimating the importance of the abortion debate.'[15]

In a movement containing so many diverse forces, how could there *not* be pro-life feminists? The strength in unity that should underpin feminism is lost when a Specific Issue Antagonist[16] such as the pro-life woman is dismissed as an invalid feminist by pro-choice women, who, in this age, are in the majority (As we will show, this was not always the case).

Criticisms of reproductive technology have been made by feminists. But, apart from the work of feminists who call themselves anti-abortion or pro-life (therefore laying themselves wide open to the sort of attacks described above), criticism of abortion within feminist discourse, probably for that very reason, has been tentative. But even among women who would call themselves 'pro-choice' feminists, a significant discomfort with abortion is frequently revealed.

Even Simone de Beauvoir's functionalist arguments for legalization of abortion, made in 1949, which called for acceptance of abortion as 'one of the risks normally implied in woman's situation',[17] nevertheless gave so many examples of the pain and sorrow and trauma of the abortion experience that it seems that any woman reading her words would be surely dissuaded from ever considering abortion.

Naomi Wolf, as another, more recent example, almost breathlessly reiterates the 'achievements' of abortion rights campaigns throughout her 'power feminism' tome *Fire with Fire*. But she admits that she is uncomfortable with much of pro-choice rhetoric, mortally afraid of 'needing' to have an abortion and desperate not to have to 'make that choice'. Her brain tells her body, 'Careful, careful. . . . *This is a matter of life and death*' (her own italics).[18] She has also referred to 'the tragedy of abortion', and describes the truism that a woman is not a feminist unless she is pro-choice as 'one of the most debilitating legacies of the reproductive choice battles of the 1980s'.[19]

Wolf wrote an article further expressing her reservations about pro-choice rhetoric (not abortion *per se*; Wolf insists that women must have 'abortion rights') in the American journal the *New Republic*.[20] Following this, she was harangued in the British press, the most voracious example being a double-act of Angela Neustatter and Maureen Freely in the *Guardian* newspaper, who together attacked Wolf's lifestyle and personal beauty, as well as her audacity to engage in free speech within feminism and the public arena about this issue,[21] and all because she acknowledged that abortion is a grave moral issue.

This is representative of the way abortion has become a sacred cow of the feminist movement. Wolf herself surmised that:

> There is a new generation of young British women that should be emerging now to take over the reins of debate over the future of feminism [in Britain] — and too many are reluctant to do so. When I ask why, many cite their terror of the routine vilification and distortion of their positions that feminists undergo in the British Press.[22]

She further mourns, 'When sexist male editors are not slamming and trivializing feminist debate, some feminist women too often gleefully take up the dirty job.' Neustatter, and others, in effect dictate that women shut up about the problem of abortion in order to keep it available for those who might want it. Abortion has therefore become more important than a woman's right to freedom of speech or thought. There are other examples: Readers of *Everywoman*, the British feminist journal, were instructed not to make any criticism of abortion because to do so would place abortion 'in a bad light'.[23] Rene Denfeld incredulously declares, 'Today's feminists are promoting man-hating, separatism and a stringent sexual morality . . . [Catherine] Mackinnon [has] gone so far as to question the right to abortion because the option of ending a pregnancy may lead to more casual sex between women and men.'[24] Denfeld's disapproval of Mackinnon is remarkably ironic because it is not the act of abortion itself, i.e. the ending the life of a foetus that Mackinnon has condemned, but only the way abortion causes women other problems.[25] Furthermore, like others, some of her criticisms of pro-choice rhetoric have apparently been made only in order to find more efficient ways of putting pro-abortion arguments across in law and the public arena.[26]

A FEMINIST CRITIQUE OF ABORTION

'Pro-life' feminist criticisms are much stronger than those described above. The feminist who, through personal experience or witness of abortion, or through a fuller understanding of the facts of abortion (currently denied to many women), becomes specifically anti-abortion, liberates herself from the pro-abortion orthodoxy that seems to have placed such a stranglehold on second-wave feminism.

But as this book explores the weakness of abortion advocacy within feminism, as we make a rigorous critique of the rhetoric of choice from a feminist perspective, we cannot proceed without care. Our disapproval of abortion relates to two factors: the certain killing of a pre-born child, and the possible, often probable physical and psychological harm inflicted on a woman. By looking at abortion in these terms, we find that we are often making a critique of a science, abortion as a technique of medical technology, a 'technical fix'.

Sandra Harding identifies two main feminist approaches to a critique of science: feminist empiricism (critique of bad science) and feminist standpoint (critique of science as usual). Feminist empiricism identifies the failure of scientists to follow principles of neutrality and objectivity in their methods. The feminist standpoint takes science itself to be problematic, for example placing it within a context shaped by cultural factors and power relations. She also argues that few feminist works fall easily into one or the other.[27] Deborah Lynn Steinberg applies this analysis with regard to the subject of *in vitro* fertilization (or IVF).[28] But even as this book is dedicated to a critique of abortion, we can also affirm that Steinberg's comments are very relevant here. Some works posit that only women who might or do undergo IVF have any stake in it. But

Steinberg argues that all women are implicated in the development of medical scientific practices which are directed towards women. I would argue, as Oakley has done,[29] that this argument applies to abortion as well. In particular, women who argue against abortion, even those who have never undergone abortion, are doing so because they are affected by its' implications, as are all women.

Abortion is often taken by its advocates as value neutral, potentially beneficial to all women. Its value as a 'choice' for women often means that the wishes of certain types of women may predominate and be taken as universal. The notion of 'choice' with regard to abortion only makes sense from certain positions, e.g. western, white, middle-class. Black women, for example, have described 'white' feminist preoccupation with abortion rights as having adverse implications for black women and communities.[30] In China, where International Planned Parenthood Federation funds have helped the government regime operate a coercive population control policy, for example,[31] the notion of abortion as a 'choice' for women is grossly inappropriate.

Pro-life feminists would argue that abortion is not value neutral at all. Abortion as an act and an institution is problematic for women. In parallel to the way doctors conduct IVF on women, the withholding of information from women about, for example, the adverse effects of abortion, foetal development and other facts is a key feature of the patriarchal nature of the medical profession. The pro-life feminist criticizes abortion from a standpoint position.

However, a problem with standpoint approaches themselves to science criticism, is that women can be implicitly constructed as passive victims of medical science even when the feminist author does not intend this.[32] We understand that, while our criticisms about abortion may show that many, possibly most women are not in full possession of knowledge of the facts or implications of abortion, while we contend that women are being harmed by abortion, these contentions may lead some people to take this view of our arguments. If we explain many women's experiences of abortion as being effectively 'lied to' or 'duped', it might appear that we are in danger of underestimating the complexity of women's experiences in undergoing or supporting abortion.

Steinberg brings an additional term to Harding's descriptions of feminist critiques, that of the 'anti-oppressive standpoint'. This term is intended to specifically locate a version of a feminist standpoint approach within a complex political agenda of change aimed at social justice.[33] We hope that it will become evident that we too, are examining abortion from an anti-oppressive standpoint position, one that recognizes the complex social relations of inequality which make abortion appear an appropriate 'choice' for some. We also do not want to universalize unconditionally, for example, some of the experiences described in this book. Neither are we condemning or blaming women who have undergone abortion: this, particularly, is something that we hope is evident in this work. But, there remains serious problems with abortion unaddressed within mainstream, 'pro-choice' feminism, not least that it destroys vulnerable life, that it causes suffering to many women, and is used so easily to oppress women. These problems need to be identified.

We hope that our analysis of abortion will provide a model for an analysis of power that does not set women as passive victims, but does nevertheless contextualise abortion within the complex relations of social inequality. We believe that a feminist anti-oppressive standpoint must eventually find against abortion as a valid means of controlling our fertility.

STANDPOINTS

Harding has identified that:

> The best form of feminist analysis . . . insists that the inquirer her/himself be placed in the same critical plane as the subject matter . . . That is, class, race, culture and gender assumptions, beliefs, and behaviours of the researcher her/himself must be placed within the frame of the picture that she/he wishes to paint.[34]

Some of the contributors to this work offer their standpoints for scrutiny, sometimes almost unconsciously understanding that the introduction of this 'subjective element' is indeed to increase objectivity by showing the whole picture. Ann Farmer takes us back to her working-class childhood and how it helped shape her socialism. Marie Claire Darke shares with us her experience of confronting the prejudices of others about her family. Ali Browning tells of childhood discoveries that shaped her adult principles. Catherine Spencer privileges us with a personal narrative which transcends the dogma and self-righteousness so often presented in what passes for debate about abortion.

In the spirit of this book, it seems only proper that I too should offer my own standpoint for scrutiny. My own opposition to abortion, contrary to probable opinion, does not consciously stem from my Catholic childhood, as I 'lapsed' in my late teens, discovering feminism at the same time. That is not to say that my worldview, my own spiritual engagements, have not been affected by Catholicism on an unconscious level: in particular, I can with hindsight link my lifelong socialism, my early committment to the peace movement, my consistent belief in an intrinsic value of life (as opposed to a 'sanctity' of life) with the positive influence of a Roman Catholic single-sex comprehensive in which a humanitarian Catholicism was taken from the assembly hall into the psyches of many young women, and from there, into political and humantiarian movements (as well as charitable and religious work for some).

But the full horror of abortion itself was brought home to me on a routine morning in an operating room where I was working as a student nurse. Looking back, I must have been more naive than I realized, because I had no idea what operations were being carried out on this gynaecological consultant's list: not until I saw the cotton netting in the suction machine fill up with blood, and something else. The senior nurse gave me the suction jar to take to the sluice room, where a fascinated medical student spread the contents over the sink, piecing together a tiny skeleton; thorax, pelvis, backbone, skull, legs and arms, to ensure nothing was left in the patient's uterus. As this pathetic skeleton lay on the sink, I could not help but see a baby, and despite the rhetoric of those who might tell me it is no such thing, the image remains with me: a dismembered baby.

I saw further abortions, including a late abortion. The days in that operating theatre were very harrowing, and affected my whole life. I wondered if the women, some thirteen-year-old victims of incest, knew what was happening to them, whether they were actually being given any 'choice' at all. My own understanding of how absurd the rhetoric of choice really is occurred through my own subsequent unplanned pregnancy. Without financial support, and under pressure to abort from many sources, the feeling of being carried on a wave to the abortion clinic was acute, and terrifying, because I felt a great love for the foetus I was carrying even hough I did not want to be pregnant.

But I resisted abortion. The foetus became a beautiful girl, and another unplanned pregnancy became a beautiful boy (even pro-life women have un-planned pregnancies!). I began to question abortion advocacy from my own feminist standpoint, a journey of enquiry that I am still travelling on. I am not alone, and neither am I the first.

A BRIEF OVERVIEW OF THE PRO-LIFE FEMINIST MOVEMENT

There is a history of pro-life feminism. But it is a hidden history which is only now beginning to be uncovered. This overview of pro-life feminism and its history has its roots in the seventies, about the same time as abortion advocacy became prevalent within what has become known as 'second wave feminism', But before then, there were pro-abortion movements not necessarily concerned for women's rights.[35] Before then, when the first feminists began to campaign against women's oppression, they were mostly 'anti-abortion'.[36]

And in the seventies, while feminism began to pervade women's conscious-ness, while goals important to all women were achieved, such as the Sex Discrimination Act in Britain, for example, while women worked towards these achievements, some of those women, feminists, on both sides of the Atlantic and elsewhere, found they could not support abortion as a feminist goal. In the US, Feminists for Life was started in 1975 by two feminists, Pat Goltz and Cathy Callaghan, dissatisfied with the pro-abortion stance of existing women's rights group there at the time. Nationwide local chapters eventually joined in a coalition, Feminists for Life of America,[37] which remains a very active and successful organization today. More recently, in 1992, the Irish group Feminists for life was started in Dublin, independently of the US movement.[38] Britain's Women for Life was started in 1975, and was active until the mid-eighties, campaigning on many women's rights, peace and justice issues. In the late eighties and early nineties, the group Feminists against Eugenics campaigned on issues which they broadly linked to eugenic attitudes, such as abortion, euthanasia, poverty, racism, pre-natal testing for gender and disability, and the death penalty.[39]

Irish, British and North American feminists are now forging links with each other. Recently, the Feminism and Non-Violence Studies Association has produced *Studies in Pro-Life Feminism*, an academic journal which is providing a forum for pro-life feminist discourse denied us by 'mainstream' feminism.[40]

Such groups have fitted into a tradition with other groups, not primarily feminist in mandate but within the same tradition of civil rights campaigns, which recognize that an advocacy of women's rights is essential to promote peace and justice and end oppression and violence. The Seamless Garment Network is a coalition of many such groups and individuals. They state that:

> We, the undersigned, are committed to the protection of life which is threatened in today's world by war, abortion, poverty, racism, the arms race, the death penalty, and euthanasia. We believe these issues are linked under a consistent ethic of life. We challenge those working on all or some of these issues to maintain a cooperative spirit of peace, reconciliation, and respect in protecting the unprotected.

Signatories include the poet Maya Angelou, and the 1976 Nobel Prize Laureate Mairead Corrigan.[41] Examples of single organizations, who most definitely cannot be associated with neoliberal or patriarchal values, include the US group Pro-Life Alliance of Gays and Lesbians (known as PLAGAL),[42] and in Britain, The Labour Life Group, which campaigns within the Labour Party.[43] Some pro-life feminists link concern about foetuses and women to concern with all life, so that abortion is linked to the exploitation of animals, and with the destruction of the environment.[44]

There are also such groups in Australasia and Canada. Whether such groups exist or could be formed in Europe, Eastern Europe, the Far East, the Third World, or other regions is not yet known, though, on the experience of countries where there is an established feminist presence, it is reasonable to presume they might. In any case, there is certainly scope for a feminist research project to find out!

PRE-EMPTION OF PRO-LIFE FEMINIST ARGUMENTS

It has been almost impossible for pro-life feminists views to be expressed in the arena in which we find ourselves. Few feminist arguments against abortion have been heard in the mainstream press or media. Therefore, our arguments are not really known. But this has not stopped abortion advocates attempting to pre-empt our arguments. Sweeping, inaccurate statements are often made about women who cannot see the act of abortion as liberating. Some less vicious assumptions about pro-life women (or any anti-abortionists, for that matter) are that they are; motivated by religion, a belief in the 'sanctity-of-life'; that they see the foetus as a 'gift', mostly from God; that they are biologically determinist,[45] that they are neoliberal, even when they profess socialist or feminist beliefs as a *root* of their opposition to abortion.[46] Commonly they are accused of suffering from 'false consciousness'.[47]

There just is not enough room in a book such as this to counter every unfair, or inaccurate, or spurious claim that has been made about pro-life women. But an acknowledgement that this has been a too-frequent occurrence is necessary, particularly as the underlying conditions for such sophistry to flourish has been the suppression of pro-life discourse in the liberal, feminist and socialist arena. An awareness of this sorry state of affairs points to the reason such a book as this is so desperately needed. Stanley and Wise criticize the 'positivist' approach of some feminist researchers who, believing they have found 'the truth', set out 'the truth about other people's lives for them',[48] a criticism often made by feminists of male scientific and other narratives. If pro-life women may only be included in feminist discourse in the third person, then feminists are guilty of that same positivism. Pro-life feminist narratives in the first person are needed within feminist discourse, to achieve the truth that feminists search for; the wider, truer picture.This book is the first in Ireland or Britain, of many such narratives, we hope. If it seems partisan (as indeed it has been described by some) then it is necessarily so. For far too long pro-abortion dogma has been allowed to dominate feminism, bringing many problems in its' wake, for women, and for the move-ment. Feminist appraisals of abortion that do not shy from voicing disapproval are necessary, not only to rectify a glaring inconsistency of feminist standpoint discourse, but also to give any woman the opportunity to appraise what might actually be wrong with abortion.

NOTES

1 Harding, S. (ed.), 'Is There a Feminist Method?' in *Feminism and Methodology* (Indiana University Press, Indiana, 1987).
2 Greer, G., 'The Cost is to Get Shafted', *The Guardian*, 23 September 1993.
3 Mann, N., 'Women on the Move', *New Statesman & Society*, 3 March 1995.
4 In Backlash (Vintage, London, 1993), for example, Susan Faludi presents an interesting analysis of the 'New Right', but appears unaware of how it may have capitalised on some of feminism's own problems, a possibility acknowledged by Rosalind Pollack Petchesky in 'Anti-abortion, Antifeminism and the Rise of the New Right' in *Feminist Studies*, vol. 7 no. 2, Summer 1981, 206–46.

5 For example, Katie Roiphe's, *The Morning After: Sex, Fear, and Feminism* (Harper Collins, London 1993).

6 See, for example, Rene Denfeld's, *The New Victorians: A Young Woman's Challenge to the Feminist Order* (Simon and Schuster, London 1995), 27. Denfeld herself is a passionate supporter of abortion, describing it as a 'medical need'. She also appears to take exception to many other feminist concerns, so that animal rights feminists are blamed by her for revealing the inconsistency of respecting animal life while disregarding foetal life and therefore weakening abortion rights arguments; and those who criticize pornography and prostitution or who analyse oppressive power-relations in heterosexuality are demonised as 'The New Victorians'.

7 References to pro-life women being 'anti-feminist' are frequent in Robin Rowland's, *Women Who Do and Women Who Don't Join the Women's Movement* (Routledge Kegan Paul, London, 1984).

8 See, for example, Ellen Willis's, 'Feminism, Moralism and Pornography' in Snitow, A. Stansell, C. and Thompson, S. (eds.) *Powers of Desire: The Politics of Sexuality* (New Feminist Library, New York, 1993), 467.

9 Bottcher, R., 'Pro-Abortion Poisons Feminism' in Grenier Sweet, G. (ed.), *Pro-life Feminism: Different Voices* (Life Cycle Books, Toronto, 1985), 45–7.

10 Rowlands, op. cit., Many contributors to this book who are implied as antifeminist give reasons such as these for not supporting feminism .

11 For Steinem's book *Outrageous Acts and Everyday Rebellions* (Flamingo, London, 1985), Fonda's front cover eulogy remains focused within Fonda's own passions: 'A book which exercises our minds while it touches our hearts.'

12 In *Sex, Art, and American Culture* (Penguin, London, 1993, 89), Paglia eulogises 'unmarried or childless women' who, due to more time and energy, are able to 'outshine and outstrip those with household responsibilities'. A dialogue between her and Sonia Friedman goes as follows: Paglia: 'All rape is erotic. All rape is sexual.' / Friedman: 'Erotic for whom?' / Paglia: Erotic for the man!' (page 71). And lastly, her view of pregnancy, 'Biologically, the female is impelled towards waiting, expectancy; her moral danger is stasis. Androgen agitates; estrogen [*sic*] tranquilizes – hence the drowsiness and the glow of pregnancy' (page 108).

13 Kates Shulman, A., 'Dancing in the Revolution: Emma Goldman's Feminism', *Socialist Review*, No. 62 , March / April 1982, 32–3.

14 Eisenstein, H., *Contemporary Feminist Thought* (Unwin Paperbacks, Sydney, 1984), xviii.

15 Rowlands, 18.

16 Rowlands, 225. The author appears to have coined this phrase to describe women who oppose the 'liberation movement' on one topic alone. Yet she too, lumps them in with 'antifeminists'.

17 de Beauvoir, S., *The Second Sex* (Penguin, London, 1983), 508.

18 Wolf, N., *Fire with Fire* (Chatto and Windus, London, 1993), 140.

19 ibid., 139.

20 Wolf, N., 'Our Bodies, Our Souls', *New Republic*, 16 October 1995.

21 'Motormouth with a B-Plus Brain' by Maureen Freely, and 'Howling Wolf', by Angela Neustatter; both appeared in the *The Guardian*, 10 October 1995.

22 'The Lady's Not for Turning', *The Guardian*, 16 October 1995.

23 Letter from Janet Hadley, *Everywoman*, July 1994.

24 Denfeld, R., op. cit.

25 MacKinnon, C., *Feminism Unmodified: Discourses on Life and Law* (Harvard Press, New York, 1987).

26 MacKinnon, C., 'Reflections on Sex Equality Under Law', *Yale Law Journal*, No. 1281, 1991.

27 Harding, S., *Whose Science? Whose Knowledge? Thinking from Women's Lives* (Open University Press, Milton Keynes, 1991).

28 Steinberg, D.L., 'Power, Positionality and Epistemology: an Anti-Oppressive Standpoint Approach', *Women: A Cultural Review*, Vol. 5 No. 3, 1994.

29 Oakley, A., 'Interviewing Women: A Contradiction in Terms', in Helen Roberts (ed.), *Doing Feminist Research* (Routledge, London 1981).

30 See, for examples, Bryan, B., Dadzie, S. and Scafe, S., *The Heart of the Race: Black Women's Lives in Britain* (Virago, London, 1985),104–5, and Bobbi Sykes in Rowlands, op. cit., 63–9.
31 Kasun, J., *The War against Population: The Economics and Ideology of Population Control* (Ignatius Press, San Francisco, 1988), 90.
32 Steinberg, as note 28, 299 .
33 Steinberg, 304.
34 Harding, S., 1987, op cit., 9.
35 Walby, S., *Theorizing Patriarchy* (Blackwell, Oxford, 1990), 80.
36 This is elaborated in chapter 1.
37 Von Koch, C., 'Reflecting as FFL Celebrates Its Tenth Birthday' in Grenier Sweet, (ed.), op. cit., 17–23.
38 Feminists for Life of Ireland can be contacted at 94 Mulvey Park, Windy Arbour, Dublin 14, Ireland.
39 Kennedy, A., 'The Heretics with a Stake in Life', *New Statesman & Society*, 21 August 1992, 20–1.
40 The Feminism and Non-Violence Studies Association can be contacted at 811 East 47th Street, Kansas City, MO 64110, USA.
41 The Seamless Garment Network can be contacted at 109 Pickwick Drive, Rochester, NY 14618, USA.
42 PLAGAL can be contacted at P.O. Box 33292, Washington, DC 20033, USA or on the internet: plagalone@aol.com.
43 The Labour Life Group can be contacted at Ashdale, Lower Oakley, Diss, Norfolk, IP21 4AP.
44 See, for example, Evans, R., 'Pro-Life, Pro-Animal, Pro-Environment Movement', *Harmony Magazine*, July 1993. *Harmony* is published by Sea Fog Press, San Francisco, A94121–0056 USA.
45 Examples of such assumptions can be found in Luker, K. 'Abortion and the Meaning of Life' in Callaghan, D. and Callaghan S., *Abortion: Understanding Differences* (Plenum Press, New York, 1984), and even in Laurie Shage's assumptions of pro-life and pro-choice standpoints in *Moral Dilemmas of Feminism* (Routledge, London, 1994). It should be noted, however, that Shage endeavours to apply consistency in her understanding of standpoint criticism, by her appreciation of how a pro-choice standpoint may actually bias or prejudice the work of commentators or researchers such as herself or Luker, and others (this is discussed further in the conclusion).
46 Stanley, L. Wise, S., *Breaking Out Again* (Routledge, London 1993), 17. The authors express the fear that some feminists label women as having 'false consciousness' if they do not accept what those feminists posit as 'the truth'.
47 The notion that any anti-abortion tendencies are part of a 'New Right' agenda is a very common assumption present in left-wing commentaries on neoliberalism.
48 Stanley and Wise, op. cit., 17.

A Lost Source of Strength and Power: The Long Feminist Tradition of Non-violent Response to Crisis Pregnancy

MARY KRANE DERR

If we live in a society where women's knowledge and theories are notable by their absence, in which women' ideas are neither respected nor preserved, it is not because women have not produced valuable cultural forms but because what they have produced has been perceived as dangerous by those who have the power to suppress and remove evidence ... So while men proceed on their developmental way building on their inherited tradition, women are confined to cycles of lost and found, only to be lost and found again – and again ... We can see that what we are doing today is not something new but something old: this is a source of strength and power.

Dale Spender, *Feminist Theorists: Three Centuries of Key Women Thinkers* (1983)

When a man steals to satisfy hunger, we may safely conclude that there is something wrong in society – so when a woman destroys the life of her unborn child, it is an evidence that either by education or circumstances she has been greatly wronged. But the question now seems to be, how shall we prevent this destruction of life and health? Mrs Stanton has many times ably answered it: 'by the true education and independence of woman.'

Mattie Brinkerhoff, nineteenth-century suffragist, in the pages of *The Revolution*, the newspaper published by Susan B. Anthony and Elizabeth Cady Stanton (1869).

The present-day war over abortion leaves the distinct impression that we may not affirm women's full personhood, especially their sexual well-being and their capacity as moral agents, without dismissing unborn children as clumps of insensate tissue. Nor may we affirm the right of unborn babies to live without trivializing the suffering that pregnancy can occasion in women's lives, or, worse, proclaiming that they *deserve* such suffering for their sexual 'wickedness'. Like the purported 'choice' between abortion and childbirth itself, this sidetaking is forced by a (so-called) civilization stuck in violent 'answers' to difficult, complex matters of social justice. It mutilates the intelligence and compassion of those who see no other way to deal with the abortion issue. Even worse, it leaves the root causes of abortion untouched. The number of dead children and wounded women continues to climb, year after year, while one group of partisans screams 'baby killers' and 'whores' and the other screams back, 'sexist, born-again bigots'.

Is there another approach to the abortion issue which will reduce rather than accelerate the number of casualties? The long, incompletely remembered history of the feminist movement offers some intriguing possibilities. For almost all of the past two centuries, women's rights activists on both sides of the Atlantic have united in the belief that abortion is a grave wrong against foetal lives which originates in grave wrongs against female lives. Feminism was not linked with abortion advocacy on a wide scale until the 1960s. Even during the past three decades a steadily growing, though often overlooked, minority of feminists has challenged the equation of the two causes.

The pro-life strain within feminism goes at least as far back as Mary Wollstonecraft, whose 1792 *Vindication of the Rights of Women* inspired the beginnings of organized feminism in both Europe and the US. She was a highly intelligent and expressive woman with a penetrating critique of gender relations. Especially after she bore an 'illegitimate' child, many dismissed her as 'immoral' – that ancient slur against 'uppity' women.

Nevertheless, she found an audience who readily discerned how her message applied to their own lives. In the *Vindication*, Wollstonecraft described how male sexual exploitation caused women to be 'weaker in mind and body than they ought to be'. As a result, they 'have not sufficient strength to discharge the first duty of a mother' and 'either destroy the embryo in the womb, or cast it off when born'. Women could be strong enough to preserve and care for their children's lives, prenatally and postnatally, if they were not undermined by their subjugation to men. In this analysis, still remarkably apt, abortion is not an assertion of woman's power but an emblem of her powerlessness.[1] Wollstonecraft was one in a long line of bravely subversive women who have been remembered for everything *but* their woman-sensitive opposition to abortion – if they have been remembered at all.

Amnesia about the tradition of pro-life sentiment within feminism is truly profound; hence the surprise of many readers when they discover an example of it in such a readily available and well known work as the *Vindication*. If present-day scholars and activists have been so determined to reclaim the long history of the struggle for gender justice, why has this amnesia come about? Today's feminists have purposefully sought and often found the inspiring assurance that their own struggles in such areas as law, education, work, spirituality, and sexuality are of a piece with the courageous and creative efforts of women past. Despite the importance that the present day feminist movement has placed on abortion, little to nothing is said about the activism of earlier women regarding this issue. Why is it so seldom mentioned?

Within the present wave of feminism, the majority have insistently defined access to abortion as a necessary precondition of women's equality, even of their very right to life itself. Because of the considerable oppression facing those who bear and/or rear children, the option to abort is viewed as an indispensable form of self-defence for women in crisis pregnancies. In the US the Fund for the Feminist Majority widely distributed a video tellingly called 'Abortion for survival'. A photograph of marchers shows the slogan 'A Woman's Right to Abortion is Akin to Her Right to Be'.[2] These slogans unmistakably imply that abortion opponents *by definition* have a death wish against women.

This version of feminism draws many women who seek validation and healing for the very real wounds they have suffered under patriarchy. These include domestic violence, rape, incest, child abuse, and most of all abortion, legal or illegal. From hard experience they may believe that anywhere else their hurts will be ignored, trivialized, or actively turned against them. No other seemingly safe haven is in sight besides the prominent version of feminism in our time, with its staunch attachment to abortion advocacy.

In this worldview, it is understandable why the pro-life stance of feminist foremothers would remain disavowed. An alternative feminist view of abortion might be experienced as an unbearably threatening paradox, with the power to tear one's very being apart. Perceiving such a threat, people may seek to protect themselves by denying its existence, or minimize it with an interpretation that leaves their own self-image and worldview intact and unchallenged. Ironically, these psychological processes account for a male-dominant society's 'suppression and removal' of women's 'valuable cultural forms', described by Dale Spender. Women's contributions are purposefully covered over, repudiated, trivialized, or co-opted to reinforce the status quo of gender relations. When it comes to the pro-life roots of their own movements, many pro-choice feminists have actually internalized the tools of the oppressor.

So it is no surprise that contemporary pro-life feminists are often dismissed as walking oxymorons, even when they produce clear evidence that they are following in the footsteps of women who pro-choice feminists have claimed as heroines. In 1990, Feminists for Life of America sought to run an ad in several progressive magazines. The ad featured, 'pro-woman, pro-life' quotes from such early feminists as Elizabeth Cady Stanton. Full citations were provided in the text. Some magazines doubted the authenticity of the material and refused it. Those editors brave enough to run the ad received a flurry of irate responses, replete with accusations of deception and misogyny. One letter raged that 'Feminists for Life' made as much sense as pro-Nazi Jews.

Intentionally or not, most material in the field of women's studies perpetuate this truncated version of feminism. As a rule, even historical sources completely miss out on the enduring pro-life strain within feminism. The omission has given rise to some truly ironic scenarios. At least one US abortion provider is named Elizabeth Blackwell Centre, after the first American woman to earn an MD. Yet Blackwell decided to become a doctor because of her passionate *opposition* to abortion. After learning of the New York abortionist Madame Restell, Blackwell wrote in her diary:

> The gross perversion and destruction of motherhood by the abortionist filled me with indignation, and awakened active antagonism. That the honorable [*sic*] term 'female physician' should be exclusively applied to those women who carried on this shocking trade seemed to me a horror. It was an utter degradation of what might and should become a noble position for women . . . I finally determined to do what I could do 'to redeem the hells', and especially the one form of hell thus forced upon my notice.[3]

Blackwell made her decision knowing full well that rejection and harassment would await her. She went on to found the first all-woman hospital in the US, and became known, not only as an innovative practitioner but also an educator and writer in the field of maternal and child health. In her first book, Blackwell exhorted women to understand and revere their bodies, including their bodies' ability to grow and nurture 'the first faint gleam of life, the life of the embryo, the commencement of human existence'.[4]

Blackwell's passion to educate women about their bodies had positive consequences outside the US. Her sense of mission and gratitude brought her back to England, the country of her birth, following her graduation from medical school. Elizabeth Garrett Anderson, the first Englishwoman to be an officially sanctioned healer, was inspired by a lecture that Blackwell gave.[5] Throughout her career, Blackwell openly fought the Restell Business.[6]

Perhaps the founders of the abortion centre honestly did not know quite whose history they were claiming as their own. However, other pro-choice activists have been conscious of the anti-abortion strain within feminism. Nevertheless, they appear to have purposefully minimized or distorted it – if they have chosen to reveal its existence at all. In the 1989 US Supreme Court case *Webster v. Reproductive Health Services*, 281 US historians signed an *Amicus* brief supporting the legal status quo. The brief portrayed nineteenth-century abortion opponents as reactionaries with unsavoury motives as the enforcement of oppressive gender and class roles and the repression of sexual understanding and pleasure.[7] Only one possible humanitarian motive for opposing abortion is mentioned, the wish to protect women from danger. According to the brief, the professed wish to protect unborn life is a late twentieth-century phenomenon, which functions merely as a 'surrogate for other social objectives that are no longer tolerated'.[8] Early feminists are not mentioned, except for the assertion that the burgeoning women's movement

had generated popular fears that women were departing from their purely maternal role . . . fueled by the fact that family size declined sharply in the nineteenth century . . . The women's movement . . . affirmed that women should always have the right to decide whether to bear a child and sought to enhance women's control of reproduction through 'voluntary motherhood', ideally to be achieved through periodic abstinence. Anxieties about changing family functions and gender roles were critical factors motivating the all-male legislatures that adopted restrictions on abortion.[9]

From this meagre commentary, offered without qualification, what conclusion might the reader draw about the stance of early feminists?

And yet the work of some *Webster* signators, cited throughout the brief, actually acknowledges that the same women who spoke out for voluntary motherhood, *agreed* with those anti-abortion laws.[10] Linda Gordon comments that practically all the early feminists 'condemned abortion and argued that the necessity of stopping its widespread practice was a key reason for instituting voluntary motherhood by other means'. Gordon mentions Tennessee Claflin, Victoria Woodhull, and Elizabeth Cady Stanton — well-known suffragists and sexual reformers — by name.[11]

Yet even acknowledgement of this troublesome historical material is generally brief and dismissive. Abortion opposition is now chalked up to absurdly old-fashioned or 'politically incorrect' reasons. It is presumed that the early feminists bought into a mystique of impossibly idealized motherhood: that they uniformly opposed nonprocreative intercourse, that they were concerned solely about the health dangers of abortion, now eradicated by legalization and technological advances. There is little to no delving into primary sources, that would give a rather different picture.[12]

The early feminists unquestionably did revere motherhood. The US abolitionist and suffragist Isabella Beecher Hooker wrote to her dear friend, the English philosopher John Stuart Mill, that she:

> . . . was impressed more and more with the likeness to the divine nature which woman seems to bear, in that she is more sensibly, if not more truly, a creator than man is. Add to this the more intimate fellowship with the child of her womb during the antenatal period, and the power of sympathy that comes through this, and you have given her a moral advantage that man can never have, and for which he has no equivalent or compensation.[13]

Echoing Hooker, free love advocate Victoria Woodhull assailed the tellingly named practice of confinement: forcing pregnant women out of public sight for the sake of 'decency':

> To bear a child is the most sacred and honorable mission on earth. The pregnant woman is a coworker with God in giving to the world an immortal being. Whoever makes so noble a deed a theme of vulgarity only proclaims

the foulness of his own base nature. Mothers themselves are ashamed when they ought to be proudest.[14]

Like other feminist mothers of her time, Elizabeth Cady Stanton was proudest when the culture insisted she ought to be most ashamed. After giving birth, she scandalized her neighbours by proudly raising a flag above her home.[15]

Early feminists did not accept the pieties about motherhood that belied the disempowerment of women. They were fully aware of a male-dominant cultural devaluation of motherhood, and identified abortion as its undesirable consequence. Eleanor Kirk, a journalist well-known in her day but little remembered in ours, was quite aware of the oppressive conditions under which mothers laboured. After the end of her marriage to an abusive alcoholic, she battled with poverty and sexual harassment from prospective employers. Eventually, she supported herself and her children through her writing. In a brilliant essay from Susan B. Anthony and Elizabeth Cady Stanton's newspaper *The Revolution*, Kirk wrote:

> What will become of the babies? Why don't [*sic*] somebody ask – what has become of the babies? Ask Restell and thousands of physicians, male and female, who have been engaged in their work of destruction for years. Physicians who have graduated from our first medical colleges, whose elegant equipages stand in front of Fifth Avenue mansions, who pocket a big fee and a little bundle of flesh at the same time, and nobody's the wiser, not even the husband in hosts of instances. What will become of the babies – did you ask – and you? Can you not see that the idea is to educate women that they may be self-reliant, self-sustaining, self-respected? God speed the time, for the sake of the babies. . . .[16]

As much as they valued maternity, early feminists believed in women's rights to exercise their other creative abilities. Matilda Joslyn Gage called abortion 'child-murder', and lamented that women's capacity for childbearing, 'which should be her glory', was instead treated by men 'as a disability and a crime'.[17] Gage was denied entrance to medical school because she was female, so she used her brilliant mind and passion for healing in the service of the women's movement, researching women's untold historical accomplishments, especially those related to spirituality. Gage believed that cultures which recognized women's Divine connections, including but not limited to the power of maternity, were more likely to respect women's talents and ensure women and children's well-being.[18]

As we have seen with Elizabeth Blackwell, feminist doctors were among the most outspoken opponents of abortion. Dr Charlotte Denman Lozier was a successful physician, medical professor, feminist and labour activist, as well as devoted mother and wife. Orphaned at age twelve, she initially became a schoolteacher to support her younger siblings. Lozier was acclaimed for defending a young pregnant woman and unborn child against abortion. Caroline Fuller had come to Dr Lozier seeking an abortion – apparently at the urging of her sexual partner, an older, married man, Andrew Moran. Lozier counselled against this, and offered Fuller her service to help Fuller bear the child. Moran became irate and abusive when Lozier refused the large bribe he offered. She sent for a policeman and he was arrested and charged with attempting to procure an abortion. This act was viewed as one of her many life accomplishments, as being: ' . . . not exceptional acts in her career but the consistent expression and outgrowth of her daily life'.[19] Dr Lozier's stand against Moran, and the support from feminists she received for it, point to their persistent challenges made to patriarchal strictures upon female sexuality, which they saw as causing abortion. From Wollstonecraft on, the 'double standard' became a key focus:

> Man has created a false public sentiment by giving the world a different code of morals for men and women, by which moral delinquencies which exclude women from society are not only tolerated, but deemed of little account in man.[20]

Such 'false public sentiment' put tremendous pressure upon women whose sexual partners abandoned them in the wake of a socially unsanctioned pregnancy. Dr Alice Bunker Stockham, a radical obstetrician and gynaecologist, wrote:

> What are some of the incentives to produce abortion? An unmarried woman, seduced under false representation by a man who feels no responsibility for his own offspring, suffers alone all the shame and contumely of the act, and is tempted to cause miscarriage to shield her good name.[21]

Early feminists are sometimes stereotyped as prudes, perhaps for similar reasons that anti-pornography feminists today are denounced as enemies of erotic pleasure: they too dared to extricate sexual expression from its patriarchal links to violence against women and children. They did not see women's sexual desire as shameful. Their concern was empowering women to protect themselves against sexual and reproductive damage that resulted from the exploitation, deceit and coercion typical of unequal relationships. They advocated partnerships based on mutual respect and affection, though opinions varied on whether they should be legally sanctioned, monogamous, lifelong unions. Early feminists hoped that women could fulfill their intense, complex capacity for sexual pleasure, neglected and repressed in a patriarchal culture. Elizabeth Blackwell thought sexual 'frigidity' an unhealthy, though understandable, self-defence against painful sexual encounters with men, and the terrifying prospect of crisis pregnancy.[22] In an era when women rarely spoke publicly, Victoria Woodhull thundered against the selfishness of men who sought their own orgasms without thinking of their partner's fulfillment.[23] Clearly intercourse was not seen for procreation purposes only. These abortion opponents were pioneering advocates of family planning, 'or voluntary motherhood'. To them, 'enforced motherhood' did not mean restricted access to abortion, as stated Dr Alice Bunker Stockam: 'The remedy is in the prevention of pregnancy, not in the procuring of abortion.'[24] This meant motherhood resulting from forced intercourse on women at times when they did not want to risk childbearing. A 'woman's right to her own body' was her right to be free of sexual coercion or rape, within as well as outside of marriage.

For some early feminists, this encompassed the right to choose contraceptive devices without threat of legal or social retribution. Writer Eliza Bisbee Duffy braved the risk of prosecution to declare, 'women should be left free to accept of reject motherhood' and assert that they should have knowledge of contraceptive means:

> They should have it that they may not have offspring forced upon them before they are ready for them; that the little ones may be welcomed with love, and desire . . . After a child is, no one has the right to tamper with its existence . . . My meaning shuts at once and forever to the door of abortion. But before that existence has commenced, we have a right . . . to consider whether we shall assume the responsibility of evoking such an existence.[25]

Others feared contraception would only increase male exploitation of women, given the disparity of power between the sexes. Although she approved of family limitation and affirmed women's capacity for sexual pleasure, Elizabeth Blackwell opposed contraceptives as 'artifices to indulge a husband's sensuality' which endangered women's health.[26]

While feminists disagreed over contraception, there was a powerful consensus that abortion was not an appropriate means to achieve voluntary motherhood. The evangelical-Christian temperance advocates were scandalized by Victoria Woodhull's free love views, but they shared her belief that 'every woman knows that if she were free, she would never bear an unwished-for child, nor think of murdering one before its birth.'[27]

There was also a feminist consensus about the power of education, from early childhood, to help women make voluntary and informed decisions about their sexual and reproductive lives, especially in regard to motherhood. Believing it necessary to preserve the lives and health of women, feminists braved cultural and legal strictures to publicly discuss 'indecent matters'. In the 1840s, Paulina Wright Davis used lifelike, detailed mannequins to educate women about their physiology. Some audience members fainted at this unprecedented sight, but others were inspired to take up the healing arts.[28] Thousands in the US and abroad read Alice Bunker Stockham's women's health manuals. *Tokology* was even translated into Russian by her friend Leo Tolstoy. Stockham recruited indigent women with no other economic alternatives but prostitution to sell her books door-to-door, for which she was fined under anti-obscenity laws.[29] Isabella Beecher Hooker took on a powerful, famous clergyman who had written a piece called 'fashionable murder', blaming abortions on women's desire to live a life

of ease. While opposing abortion herself, Hooker believed there was a better way
to remedy the problem:

> There is a great disinclination on the part of refined and fastidious people to
> have these subjects spoken of at all . . . but nothing is clearer to me than that
> the best welfare of our race, both moral and physical, requires that they be
> understood . . . Do we simply lop the branches and leave the sturdy trunk,
> when we criticize this and that practice of human parents, and overlook their
> fundamental misconceptions of the nature of their being? [30]

As the above example suggests, feminists believed sex education should
include information about foetal development, so that women would realize the
humanity of unborn children.[31] Eliza Duffey revealed her earlier belief that there
was no harm in abortion, as the foetus was not truly a human life. Her views
changed when 'I became thoroughly acquainted with sexual physiology, and
comprehended the wonderful economy of nature in the generation of the human
germ.' Yet she cautioned those who would condemn women contemplating
abortion:

> . . . Tell them the how and why of the whole matter, and they will discover the
> wrong themselves, and feel the full force of it, far more than they ever can by
> taking it merely on the say-so of men.[32]

This is the heart of early feminist objection to abortion: as an act of violence.
Their synonyms were not 'the right to choose' but 'child murder' and 'infanticide'. Though they were very concerned with the danger of abortion to women,
this was not their only objection.[33] Victoria Woodhull, never missing an opportunity to call a spade a spade, declared: 'The rights of children, then, as
individuals, begin while yet they are in foetal life.'[34]

Most early feminists were deeply religious, but their faiths were diverse —
from evangelical Christianity, to Quakerism, to Swedenborgian-based Spiritu-
alism to Matilda Joslyn Gage's reawakening of a past 'Matriarchate'. These faiths
motivated them to a common struggle against gender injustice. They engaged
issues rediscovered by current-wave feminists: the misinterpretation of holy
writings to bolster existing power struggles, exclusion of women from clerical
roles, the devaluation of the body in the name of 'morality', the suppression of
the feminine principle within the Divine.[35] In recognizing foetal life as human,
feminists were not attempting to impose sectarian beliefs on unwilling recipients,
but responding with wonder to new scientific information which redefined the
start of human life as the moment of conception.[36] Alice Bunker Stockham and
contemporaries such as Dr Anna Densmore French wished to supplant the
earlier belief that women had been raised on, that life did not begin until
'quickening'.[37] Early feminists would probably distrust the contemporary notion
that a biological human could still be excluded from personhood because she was
insufficiently developed. They struggled against the rationalization that women

lacked certain rights because they were biologically inferior. Like their present day descendents, some did have their moments of prejudice on the basis of class, race, sexual orientation and/or disability, moments which are not to be excused. The privileged and Caucasian Elizabeth Cady Stanton, for example, feared the reproduction of the lower classes, African Americans, and disabled persons. Such attitudes must be denounced, especially at a time when they are still very much among us. It must also be stressed, at the same time, that they were unrelated to the early feminist case against abortion. The anti-abortion stance was, rather, related to their involvement in causes such as the abolition of slavery, elimination of the death penalty and other harsh sentences, improvement of labour conditions, peace, challenging child abuse and child labour, opposing injustice against indigenous peoples, and even, in some cases, advocating vegetarianism and animal welfare.[38]

As we have seen, their anti-abortion stance was not motivated by misogyny, but compassion for pregnant women. Laura Cuppy Smith, an English immigrant to the US and associate of Victoria Woodhull, was inspired to her activism by her unmarried teenage daughter's unplanned pregnancy and their decision against abortion:

> I made my resolve. I said 'This child of youth and love! This child of my child has a right to live, and *shall* live – has a right to love, and shall have that also; has a mission to its mother and shall perform it . . . This girl-mother has a right to all tenderness . . . Love, not guilt, has made her what she is. If the world calls her 'wicked', 'outcast', the world lies, and we will live the lie down.' . . . She answered, 'Mother, you are right, and I am not afraid since you love me still' . . . For myself do you wonder that my whole life is consecrated to the cause of freedom?[39]

Smith was not the only feminist to act compassionately in such a situation, as shown by the case of Hester Vaughan, who was impregnated and then abandoned by her employer. When her child was stillborn in her unheated garrett, she was accused of infanticide and sentenced to death. Feminists, including Susan B. Anthony, Elizabeth Cady Stanton, and Eleanor Kirk campaigned successfully for leniency and for her release from prison. After, they helped the penniless Vaughan return to her relatives in England.[40] Nor were women who had resorted to abortion excluded from compassion. Elizabeth Edson Evans, a writer noted for her strong pro-life views, sympathetically presented harrowing testimonies from post-abortion women in her book *The Abuse of Maternity*,[41] as did peace activist and abolitionist Henry Clarke Wright, in his *Unwelcome Child*.[42] Writer Sarah F. Norton, who denounced abortion facilities as 'dens of deaths', called for the day when 'an unmarried woman will not be despised for her motherhood'.[43]

Feminists agitated for legislation to raise the age of consent to sexual intercourse – an effort to protect young girls from the life-altering consequences of premature, coerced sex. Urban feminists were concerned about women who moved to the cities and found few economic opportunities other than prostitution. Crisis pregnancies were common in this population. Defying the popular belief that such women were among the 'undeserving poor', feminists offered them shelter, clothing, and training in marketable job skills. In an appeal for Chicago's Anchorage Mission, one facility assisting these young women, Frances Willard asked those with material resources and happy family lives to 'remember our sisters who are in bonds, as bound with them'.[44]

Until the late 1960s, such woman-affirming opposition to abortion predominated among feminists. Some abortion advocacy did appear in the first decades of this century, most notably on the part of Canadian-born, English socialist Stella Browne. She may have been motivated by a personal experience of abortion to take up some familiar sounding arguments, beginning around 1915:

> Abortion must be a key to a new world for women . . . It should be available for any woman, without insolent inquisitions, nor ruinous financial charges, nor tangles or red tape. For our bodies are our own . . . . It is as much a woman's right as the removal of a dangerously diseased appendix.[45]

In portraying crisis pregnancy as a disease, and abortion as a liberating cure, strong enough to make 'a new world for women', Browne did not have a great deal of company. Even Browne's admiring biographer, Sheila Rowbotham, concedes this point, noting, for example, that Lady Rhondda's Six Points Group supported an anti-abortion clause in the 1924 Children and Young Persons Bill.[46] Sylvia Pankhurst's pacifism. socialism, and feminist zeal for maternal-child welfare clearly included unborn children. In midlife, Pankhurst gave birth to a child outside of legal marriage, This prompted her to write a book, *Save the Mothers*, which argued that the high rates of maternal, prenatal and postnatal mortality could be prevented if the government created a free, universal maternity service rather than squandering the money on defence. Greater access to abortion was not part of her vision:

> It is grievous indeed that the social collectivity should feel itself obliged to assist in so ugly an expedient as abortion in order to mitigate its crudest evils. The true mission of Society is to provide the conditions, legal, moral, economic and obstetric, which will assure happy and successful motherhood.[47]

Bertha Pappenheim would probably have agreed, one of the first social workers in Germany, and its leading Jewish feminist before the Nazis came to power. She is better known, however, as the patient whom Sigmund Freud and Josef Breuer identified as Anna O, the person who first referred to psychoanalysis as 'the talking cure'. She was a remarkably intelligent and spirited young woman who found no outlets for her creativity in her stiflingly orthodox environment. Breuer treated her for unexplained symptoms which he diagnosed as 'hysteria'.

After he terminated treatment in 1882, she continued to be symptomatic and was subjected to harsh interventions such as electric shock and arsenic. But Pappenheim transformed her own suffering into empathy for oppressed people. She founded the Judischer Frauenbund, a dynamic organization which sought political, economic and religious equality for Jewish women. She tirelessly provided social services to vulnerable women and children. She was especially concerned about abandoned wives and unwed mothers. It was in this context that she spoke out powerfully against prostitution and abortion. Pappenheim stated that 'the ability for assimilation of the Jewish spirit showed to its detriment' in abortion advocacy. She was worried that some Jewish feminists would unthinkingly adopt this position 'without proper criticism' and thereby 'overshadow for many women spiritual and social achievements.' When the Nazis came to power, the elderly Pappenheim helped other Jews to emigrate, until her death from cancer in 1936. Much of her life's work was wiped out in the Holocaust.[48] What shape might feminism have today if more of her work, including her holistic understanding of abortion, had survived?

Alice Paul, who lived from 1885 to 1977, bore witness to feminism's loss of its earlier wisdom regarding abortion, and it troubled her greatly. A devout Quaker, she was committed to peaceful methods of social change. She went to England and learned civil disobedience tactics practised by the suffragists there, contributing to the struggle that won US women the vote in 1920. She authored the original Equal Rights Amendment (ERA) to the US Constitution in 1923. When the current wave of feminism emerged, she was glad for its emphasis on ERA. Yet she feared that the movement's insistence on abortion 'rights' would sabotage the fight for the ERA and thus women's best interests. A few years before her death, she voiced this concern to Pat Goltz, Feminists for Life of America co-founder. Paul's fear was prophetic. Her objection to abortion has been attributed to her preference for a single-issue approach to political action. Yet it appears to have gone much deeper than that. According to her long-time colleague Evelyn Judge, Paul termed abortion 'the ultimate in the exploitation of women' and asked: 'How can one protect and help women by killing them as babies?'[49]

Younger feminists of diverse backgrounds have powerfully articulated and expanded upon such an understanding of abortion. In the 1970s Dr Constance Redbird Uri, a Cherokee-Choctaw physician, uncovered the appalling extent to which Native American women had been involuntary sterilized and forcibly aborted by the US government's Indian Health Service. She saw such practices as linked to the government's long-standing policy of decimating the Native population:

> We belong to a culture that holds all life to be sacred . . . This belief has sustained our people throughout the long struggle for survival . . . The

Whiteman's culture that kills its unborn is foreign to our way of life . . . The Whiteman's solution to the Indian Woman's poverty is to kill her unborn.[50]

The Chicana activist Graciela Olivarez also saw racism where abortion was touted as a solution to social problems. Although a high school drop-out, she became the first woman graduate from Notre Dame University Law School, the head of the Community Services under President Jimmy Carter, and a senior consultant with the United Way, one of the largest sources of private funding for charities in the US. In 1972, the year before the *Roe v. Wade* decision, she took part in President Nixon's Commission on Population and the American Future. While asserting the necessity for safe contraception, she dissented strongly with its conclusion that legalized abortion would help solve poverty and overcrowding:

> To talk about the 'wanted' and 'unwanted' child smacks too much of bigotry and prejudice. Many of us have experienced the sting of being 'unwanted' by certain segments of our society . . . Every individual has his/her rights, not the least of which is the right to life, whether born or unborn. Those with power in our society cannot be allowed to 'want' and 'unwant' people at will. I am not impressed or persuaded by those who express concern for the low-income woman who may find herself carrying an unplanned pregnancy and for the future of the unplanned child who may be deprived of the benefits of a full life because of the parent's poverty, because the fact remains that in this affluent nation of ours, pregnant cattle and horses receive better health care than pregnant, poor women . . . Medical science has developed four different ways for killing a fetus, but has not yet developed a safe-for-all-to-use contraceptive . . . As long as we continue to view abortion as a solution, we will continue to avoid facing the real issue – that abortion treats the symptom and neglects the disease . . . When you consider the current rush to reform the welfare system because the cost has gotten out of hand supposedly as a result of 'all those babies being born to lazy women', but subsidies to profit-making entities suffer not one iota, one begins to get a glimpse of the disease.[51]

The words and deeds of Uri and Olivarez resonate with those of Fannie Lou Hamer, an African-American woman who, after a white doctor forcibly sterilized her in the early 1960s, became a passionately nonviolent civil rights activist, fighting for improved government nutrition, health and education programmes. While lamenting the Vietnam War and its disproportionate number of African-American casualties, she spoke of legal abortion as 'genocide' and 'legal murder'. Hamer knew the complex issues surrounding crisis pregnancy. Her adopted, unmarried daughter had given birth to a child which Hamer adopted when her daughter died after being denied emergency treatment on the grounds of race. To the end of her own life, Hamer maintained that greater communal support was the answer to black women's reproductive dilemmas. She herself testified in court on behalf of young black women denied employment because they were single mothers, and had given at least one plaintiff financial and moral support to go to college. She felt it absurd to deny help to young women who went to term rather than aborting.[52]

The vision of pro-life feminism not only has a long and honourable history, it has become even more relevant in an era when the world is shrinking, and at such a pace. It offers hope for healing the violent polarities of the abortion debate. Indeed, it holds exceptional promise for linking women – and men – of highly diverse backgrounds. Most of all, it promises authentic, holistic solutions to all the parties involved in difficult pregnancies. It is not, nor has it ever been, 'a surrogate for other social objectives that are no longer tolerated.' Rather, it is 'a lost source of strength and power' that needs to be reclaimed and built upon – this time, on a global scale, without becoming lost again.

NOTES

1 Wollstonecraft, M., *A Vindication of the Rights of Woman* (ed.) Poston, C.H. (W.W. Norton, New York, 1975), 139.

2 Boston Women's Health Collective, *The New Our Bodies Ourselves* (Simon & Schuster, New York, 1984), 315.

3 Ross, I., *Child of Destiny: the Life Story of the First Woman Doctor* (Harper & Brothers, New York, 1949), 88.

4 Blackwell, E., *The Laws of Life* (Putnam & Sons, New York, 1852), 70–73.

5 Banks, O., *Faces of Feminism* (Basil Blackwell, London, 1986), 39.

6 Ross, op. cit., 88.

7 *William L. Webster et al. v. Reproductive Health Services*, Brief of 281 American Historians as Amici Curiae Supporting Appellees, US Supreme Court, October Term, 1988.

8 Webster Brief, 30.

9 Webster Brief, 17–19.

10 See, for example, Degler, C., *At Odds: Women and the Family in America from the Revolution to the Present* (Oxford University Press, New York, 1980); Gordon, L., *Woman's Body, Woman's Right* (Penguin Books, New York, 1976).

11 Gordon, ibid., 108.

12 Cosgrove, T., ' Distorted History', *Chicago Sun-Times*, 8 February 1991.

13 Beecher Hooker, I., *Womanhood: Its Sanctities and Fidelities* (Lee & Shepard, Boston, 1874), 33–7.

14 Victoria Woodhull, quoted in the Dubuque, *Iowa Times*, 3 February 1874.

15 Schnittman, S., 'FFL of Western New York Honors Elizabeth Cady Stanton', *American Feminist*, Spring 1996.

16 Kirk, E., 'What Will Become of the Babies', *The Revolution*, 28 May 1868.

17 Gage, M.J., 'Is Woman Her Own?', *The Revolution*, 9 April 1868.

18 See Gage, M.J., *Woman, Church, and State* (Charles Kerr, Chicago, 1893).

19 'Mrs Charlotte D. Lozier', *Home Journal*, 12 January 1870.

20 Anthony, S. B. Cady Stanton, E. and Gage, M.J. (eds.), *The History of Woman Suffrage: Volume One* (Fowler & Wells, New York, 1881), 71.

21 Stockham, A.B., *Tokology* (Sanitary Publishing Company, Chicago, 1887), 245–51. 'Tokology' is a Greek word for obstetrics.

22 Blackwell quoted in Haller, J.S. Haller R.M., *The Physician and Sexuality in Victorian America* (Norton, London, 1974), 99.

23 Woodhull quoted in Sachs, E., *The Terrible Siren* (Harper & Brothers, New York, 1928), 223–4.

24 Stockham, op. cit.

25 Duffey, E.B., 'The Limitation of Offspring', *Relations of the Sexes* (Wood & Holbrook, New York, 1876.

26 Banks, J.A., and Banks, O., *Feminism and Family Planning in Victorian England* (Schocken Books, New York, 1964), 93.

27 Victoria Woodhull, quoted in the Wheeling *West Virginia Evening Standard*, 17 November 1875.

28 Davis, P.W., *History of the National Women's Rights Movement* (Journeymen Printer's Cooperative, New York, 1871), 32.

29 Catherine Yronwode, 'Karezza and Alice Bunker Stockham', http://www.tantra.org.

30 Beecher Hooker, op. cit., 7–12, 15–16, 24–7.

31 Blackwell's, 'The Laws of Life' and Stockham's, 'Tokology' are among a number of feminist doctors' treatise which educated readers about foetal development.

32 Duffey, E.B., op. cit.

33 Degler, op. cit., 243.

34 Woodhull, V., 'The Training of Children – Good Advice to Mothers', *Woodhull & Claflin's Weekly*, 7 October 1871.

35 See, for example, Gage's *Woman, Church and State* 1893; Stanton's *The Woman's Bible* (Coalition Task Force on Women and Religion, Seattle, WA, reprinted 1974), and Braude, A., *Radical Spirits* (Beacon Press, Boston, 1989).

36 Stockham, op. cit.

37 'Lectures of Dr Anna Densmore', *The Revolution*, 19 March 1868.

38 See, for example, Degler, 247.

39 Smith, L.C., 'How One Woman Entered the Ranks of Social Reform' *Woodhull & Claflin's Weekly*, 1 March 1873.

40 See, for example, 'Elizabeth Cady Stanton', 'Hester Vaughan', *The Revolution*, 19 November 1868.

42 Evans, E.E., *The Abuse of Maternity* (J.B. Lippincott, Philadelphia, 1875).

43 Wright, H.C., *The Unwelcome Child* (Bela Marsh, Boston, 1858).

44 Norton, S.F., 'Tragedy – Social and Domestic', *Woodhull & Claflin's Weekly*, 19 November 1870.

45 Willard, F., 'A Plea for the Forgotten', *The Union Signal*, 28 November 1895.

46 Browne, S., 'The Right To Abortion', quoted in Rowbotham, S., *A New World for Women* (Pluto Press, London, 1978) 110–24.

47 Rowbotham, ibid., 34.

48 Pankhurst, E.S., 'Abortion', *Save the Mothers* (Knopf, London, 1930), 108–10.

49 Jones, E., *The Life and Work of Sigmund Freud* (Basic Books, 1953), 223–5; Edinger, D., *Bertha Pappenheim, Freud's Anna O.* (Congregation Solel, Highland Park, IL, 1968), 80 and passim.

50 Osborne, C., 'Pat Goltz, Catherine Callaghan, and the Founding of Feminists for Life', Krane Derr and M. MacNair, R., Naranjo-Heubl (eds.), *Prolife Feminism: Today and Yesterday* (Sulzberger & Graham, New York, 1995), 151–156; Harrison, C., *On Account of Sex* (University of California Press, Berkeley, 1988), 205. Gallagher, R.S., 'I Was Arrested, of Course: An Interview with Miss Alice Paul' *American Heritage*, February 1974; Evelyn K. Samras Judge, letters to Mary Krane Derr, 12 and 21 September 1989. In 1992, when Paul's house in New Jersey was declared a National Historic Landmark, Judge tried to take part in the dedication ceremony and inform the abortion advocates there that her old friend had been pro-life. She was rebuffed (see Duganitz, B., 'Alice Paul: *Reality v. Propaganda*', *Feminists for Life of Minnesota Newlsetter*, April 1992). The amnesia does not stop there. In that area of New Jersey, the National Organization for Women group characterizes abortion as a positive good. The division proudly calls itself the Alice Paul Chapter.

51 *Voices of the Indian Women* (Los Angeles: Indian Women United for Social Justice, 1970), 1;

words originally written by Redbird Uri. See also items about her work in *Indian Country Today*, 24 August 1994, and *Medical Tribune*, 24 August 1977.

52 Olivarez, G., 'Separate Statement', *Population and the American Future: the Report of the Commision on Population and the American Future* (General Accounting Office, Washington DC 1972), 160–64. Her accomplishments are recalled in Garcia Johnson, R.R., 'Graciela Olivarez (1928–1987), Government Official, Public Educator'; Telgen, D. and Kamp, J. (eds.), *Notable Hispanic American Women* (Gale Research, 1993), 300–1.
53 Hamer, F.L., 'Is It Too Late?' Speech given in 1971. Testimony of Hamer in *Katie Mae Andrews and Lestine Rogers v. Drew Separate Municipal School District*, 425 US 559, 1976. Mills, K., *This Little Light of Mine. The Life of Fannie Lou Hamer* (Dutton, New York, 1993), 274.

(*Editor's note*: It is strongly recommended that readers searching for primary resources listed within these endnotes see the anthology *Prolife Feminism: Today and Yesterday*. It is available from the publishers at 505 Eighth Avenue, 13th Floor, New York, New York, 100018 USA, e-mail address 103044.2702@compuserve. com.)

2

Empty Rhetoric: A Feminist Enquiry into Abortion Advocacy and the 'Choice' Ethic

BREDA O' BRIEN

Within the academic world of feminism there has been what Rosalind Delmar calls 'a sort of sclerosis of the movement, segments of which have become separated from and hardened against each other.'[1] Sandra Schneiders, the pro-choice Roman Catholic theologian, contents herself with describing four segments – liberal, cultural, socialist and radical feminists.[2] Others, like Delmar, say:

> Such differing explanations, such a variety of emphases in their practical campaigns, such widely varying interpretations of their results have emerged, that it now makes more sense to speak of a plurality of feminisms than of one.[3]

And yet, when Sheryl Ruzek states baldly, 'Therefore, ensuring every woman's right to abortion (whether she chooses to have one or not) is a central tenet of contemporary western feminism',[4] we appear to have a cause which unites all strands of feminism. Even the 'veteran Irish campaigner Mary Gordon' is quoted as saying:

> A measure of the strength of the feminist movement in any country is the strength and confidence of its abortion rights lobby.[5]

So, while feminism has many faces, what seems to distinguish a feminist from a non-feminist is not just the notion (to quote Delmar again), that:

> at the very least a feminist is someone who holds that women suffer discrimination because of their sex, that they have specific needs which remain negated and unsatisfied, and that the satisfaction of these needs would require a radical change (some would say a revolution even) in the social, economic and political order.[6]

No, what seems to unite all forms of feminism, from radical separatists to yuppie power feminists is the idea of a woman's right to choose, or, put less euphemistically, the idea that any woman, anywhere, in any circumstances has a right to end the life of a foetus developing inside her.

This emphasis on abortion as a 'central tenet' has, I believe, been extremely damaging for feminism. Firstly, it has tied up precious and finite resorces which could have been used in other ways. Secondly, it has meant that any women ambivalent about or opposed to abortion have ceased to feel welcome within the feminist movement, however passionate they are about justice for women. Thirdly, and most importantly, it has undermined the credibility of the women's movement as a movement for justice.

Historically, feminism has had its roots in many movements for human rights, such as the fight to end racism. Feminism grew out of a desire to end oppression of women. It would seem a great betrayal of those ideals if feminism in its turn oppresses another group in society – particularly if that group is weak and defenceless.

Paolo Freire has pointed out that every person who is oppressed has a tendency to oppress in turn, given the opportunity:

> But almost always, in the initial stage of the struggle, the oppressed, instead of striving for liberation, tend themselves to become oppressors, or 'sub-oppressors'. The very structure of their thought has been conditioned by the contradictions of the concrete existential situation by which they were shaped.[7]

Is this what has happened to the women's movement? Patriarchy is the identified enemy of justice for women. The essence of a patriarchal structure was the Roman paterfamilias. In Schneider's description:

> Thus in ancient societies, he owned wives and concubines, children, slaves, animals, land, produce and money and had not only responsibility for his property, but also absolute power over it. It was the right of the head of the household to expose unwanted infants; to sell, barter, or donate wives, children or slaves; to kill recalcitrant dependents; to acquire and alienate real and personal property.[8]

'To kill recalcitrant dependents' has a horribly familiar ring.

The whole notion of abortion as central to feminism is based on the idea that women will never be equal to men until women can be as free from the consequences of unplanned pregnancy as a man is. The odd thing about this position is that a central capability of women is seen as a handicap to be overcome, not a difference to be celebrated. Men, with their inferior reproductive capacity, are posited as the ideal to which to aspire. Unfortunately, women need surgery to aspire to that high estate. To quote Laurence Tribe:

> In addition, equality for women must mean the same ability to express human sexuality without the burden of pregnancy and childbirth, that has always

been, by accident of biology, available to men. With technology that is no longer even new, this equality is within reach.[9]

So, lie down on the table, sister, and with my scalpel and vacuum extractor I will make you as good as a man. How has it been possible for us to accept this definition of our bodies as flawed becasue of our reproductive capacities? What species of self-hatred have we internalized to believe that it is we who require surgical adjustment, not society which needs adjustment to meet 'our specific needs which remain negated and unsatisfied?' To quote Freire on the subject of internalised oppression again, perhaps a little unfairly, since this translation uses sexist language which reinforces my point more forcefully:

> Their ideal is to be men; but for them to be a 'man' is to be an oppressor. This is their model of humanity. This phenomenon derives from the fact that the oppressed, at a certain point, develop an attitude of 'adherence' to the oppressor. At this level, their perception of themselves as opposites of the oppressor does not yet signify involvement in a struggle to overcome the contradiction; the one pole aspires not to liberation, but to identification with the opposite pole.[10]

Can it be possible that women, because of centuries of oppression, have learned to despise what makes them different to men? Simone de Beauvoir pointed out how men justified their oppression of women by setting them up as the 'Other' – without rights except in relation to men. If we look at her famous statement about the 'Other' something interesting happens:

> Thus humanity is male and man defines woman not in herself but as relative to him; she is not regarded as an autonomous being. Michelet writes, 'Woman, the relative being . . .' and Benda is most positive in his *Rapport d'Uriel*: 'the body of man makes sense in itself quite apart from a woman, whereas the latter seems wanting in significance by itself . . . man can think of himself without woman. She cannot think of herself without man . . . She is denied and differentiated with reference to man and not he with reference to her; she is the incidental, the inessential as opposed to the essential. He is the Subject, he is the Absolute – she is the Other.[11]

It seems outrageous. How dare men imagine that they are the definition of humanity, that the male body makes sense in and of itself while the body of a woman is somehow lacking? Yet, if you substitute unborn child for the word 'she' and woman for 'man', look what happens:

> The body of woman makes sense in itself quite apart from an unborn child, whereas the latter seems wanting in significance by itself . . . woman can think of herself without the unborn child. The unborn child cannot think of herself without the woman . . . The unborn child is denied and differentiated with

reference to woman and not woman with reference to the unborn child; the unborn child is the incidental, the inessential as opposed to the essential. Woman is the Subject, woman is the Absolute – the unborn child is the Other.

Exactly the same logic, with exactly the same consequences – oppression.

No doubt this will spark fury in abortion advocates. How dare I compare a completely dependent foetus with a fully grown autonomous woman, and say their rights are equal. Yet it is only in a culture where independence is the ultimate value (and consumerist choice an expression of that value) that dependency becomes a crime punishable by ending the life of the dependent one. Since when has individualism and consumer culture been the guiding philosophy of feminism? What of the much vaunted 'female' values of interdependence and co-operation?

A right to abortion can only be justified if the developing member of the next generation has no rights in comparison with those of a more developed adult. It means ignoring, diminishing, dengrating that member of the next generation in terms very similar to those used for centuries to justify the oppression of women; 'weak' . . . 'immature' . . . 'incapable of survival' . . . 'parasitic' . . . 'dependent'.

Yet, if you consider that we all started life in that way, and only became adults because a woman did not see our dependency as a disease requiring termination, such language begins to appear very strange. If you consider how short in duration is this technical condition of dependence prior to so-called viability, it begins to look even more strange. A vet who put down your pet and then casually informed you 'if I had waited a few weeks or months you would have had a perfectly healthy animal' would probably be struck off. Yet doctors abort foetuses all the time who would obtain viability in a matter of weeks. (Women in the real world know that viability is a purely medical term. How 'viable' is a three-year-old without constant supervision and care, for example?)

Kathleen Barry has some trenchant things to say about the techniques used to subjugate women and keep them in prostitution:

> In otherness, time is made to stand still for the oppressed. By representing the oppressed as biologically or culturally different, by reducing them by means of their difference to 'others', patriarchial power dismembers women from their history. *That is how human beings are deprived of their humanity* (italics mine).[12]

Care is always taken to divert attention from the nature of what or whom is being aborted. This is precisely what happens when terms such as 'a blob if cells' are used of an embryo or foetus. What woman, whether happy about her pregnancy or not, ever announced, 'I'm expecting a blob of cells'? Every woman intuitively knows the humanity of the small creature within her, and the consequences of acknowledging that humanity. From the moment a woman knows she is pregnant she begins to think in the future tense. If she is working outside the home, she thinks of the effects on her career, on her prospects for maternity leave. If she has other children, she thinks of the effects on them. If she has a partner, she thinks about the effect on the relationship. And in each of these internal conversations, it is a baby of whom she is thinking. Carol Gilligan is right when she says that women think in terms of relationships,[13] but wrong, however, in the weight which she thinks women give to the most primal of relationships, – that between a woman and the baby she is carrying. Those feminists who speculate that patriarchy arose from men's desire to control the uncanny power which women have in bearing the next generation, seem to have fallen into a very patriarchal denigration of that function. Naturally, we are not solely defined by our biology, but we are not degraded and burdened by it, except when society refuses us adequate respect and support.

Kathleen Barry continues, in relation to the subjugation of women:

> Sexual oppression, through its biological determinisms, halts women's forward movement and thereby attempts to annihilate the possibilities of their progress, change, growth and development . . . Oppression is a historical condition in which, for the oppressed, time is shrunk to the moment; for that is what it means to be ahistorical, outside of time, immanent and therefore not transcendent.[14]

Nothing changes more rapidly than a child in the womb. It has been pointed out that were the foetus to maintain the same level of growth as it has in the first few weeks, human infants would be the size of baby elephants when delivered. We cannot claim to be unaware that she or he is more than just a 'blob'. Lennart Nilson[16] and ultrasound have deprived us of that evasion.

Precisely what Barry says about women who are oppressed is true of humans in the womb. If we render them ahistorical, situate them outside the possibility of change and development, we can then abuse them. Once we acknowledge that they are in process just as those outside the womb, we can no longer justify their termination. This is not to say that those in the womb are merely potential human beings, but, that they are human beings in the first stage of incredible development which abortion would seek to deny them. Those rights to grow and change can only be denied by viewing the foetus or embryo as static and not in process, by annihilating 'the possibilities of their progress, change, growth and development.'

I feel it is important to state at this point that I am attacking the philosophical underpinnings of feminist advocacy of abortion, not women who have had abortions. There is, usually, so much pain in the decision to abort, I would not willingly add to it. However, I would like to undermine the ideology which told women that it was of no more significance than a tonsillectomy, in a glorious example of how women's lived experience can be totally ignored when it does not fit with the prevailing orthodoxy (even if that orthodoxy is radical feminism).

Barry, a writer whom I greatly admire for the moral fervour with which she has championed the rights of women who are prostitutes in the face of much opposition, including from pro-pornography, pro-prostitution feminism, has some interesting things to say on the reification of choice as the ultimate value. She is speaking in the context of feminists who are pro-prostitution, but I feel it has important implications for women who are pro-abortion:

> This is a variant of liberal ideology, which drives economic markets by elevating individual choice in order to maximise consumerism. In this way, the sex of prostitution is reduced from being a class condition of women to a personal choice of the individual. Under the decadence that elevates personal choice above the common good, chosen patriarchal violation serves capitalist market exchange.[17]

This also applies to abortion. If you elevate personal choice above the common good, you consciously decide to ignore the rights of developing human beings simply becasue they are smaller, weaker and more dependent. In short, you enshrine patriarchal values at the heart of feminism.

The reification of personal choice in abortion consciously excludes whole areas of concern from consideration. The whole language of choice in relation to abortion is all to do with a woman choosing what is 'right' for her – with no other referents. This is shown particularly clearly in those feminist writings which actually acknowledge a right to life of the unborn:

> For Irish women choosing termination, and given our particular cultural heritage, moral exercise is located in a prima facie right to life of the unborn which may only be over-ridden with justification, or good reason *to be provided by the woman herself* [emphasis mine.][18]

But wait a minute – what other 'prima facie right to life' should be 'over-ridden' because of reasons provided by the person about to do the 'over-riding'? Take the prima facie right to life of a woman about to be beaten by her husband. Would you accept his reasons for 'over-riding' her rights?

The 'respect for women as moral agents' argument presumes that the decisions take place within a moral vacuum. Any decision which a woman makes which is 'right for her' is automatically right. this seems to overlook the possibility that a moral agent (even if that agent is a woman) also has the ability to make bad choices, decisions that are not morally correct. It seems that men can make moral choices that are automatically wrong and deserving of moral censure (for example, rape, or acting out of a patriachal mindset which oppresses women) but women can only make moral choices which are worthy of approval, provided they are 'right for her'.

This is feminist Lesley Saunders' account of the abortion of her fourth child, after a miscarriage and two children brought to term. She decided to have an abortion so that she could write a book:

For me, whose other children before their births had mapped the inner landscapes of reality with their quite definite dimensions, there was no question but that abortion was killing. I knew that, as I knew I had to make peace with the child I did not want. Other women may think and feel differently. I promised her — both M and I felt the child to be female — that her life-spark would somehow re-enter mine. I would take responsibility for carrying through the meaning of her life. I would dedicate her creative life to her because she had given up her life for me, in order that I could mother myself instead of her. The decision was hard to make . . . .

Lesley had been ambivalent about becoming a parent and therefore careless about contraception. She requests a local anaesthetic for the abortion:

It was painful and shocking. Not as painful as birth, but sharper, where I couldn't get at it. I just kept saying 'Bye bye baby, bye bye baby,' letting the pain out in soft moans as the instruments went in and after an age, came out again. Afterwards I curled in the recovery room like a foetus myself, full of hurt.[19]

Lesley Saunders dedicated her book *Glancing Fires* to the daughter she aborted.

We are expected to apply none of the moral criteria normally applicable when a person consciously kills another to improve their own circumstances, because it is a woman organising the killing of a foetus in her womb. Imagine, if she were speaking of a six-month-old baby, an elderly mother, or her partner. Imagine if her partner had desided to terminate Lesley. All of those actions would be found morally reprehensible, but not Lesley's decision, because it is her 'right to choose'. To accord her decision anything but unqualified approval is to be that dread of the politically correct, 'judgemental'. And yet isn't one of the conseqe-unces of liberation the ability to exercise judgement? There is another judge-ment; of a system that allowed a woman in comfortable circumstances and a stable relationship to abort a child so that she could write a book, without once questioning the morality of her actions.

The book in which this account is found is written by four women. There is evidence that some of those women were so unenlightened as to query whether a freely chosen abortion as described by Lesley Saunders is of the same order of experience as the other pregnancy losses:

An important feature of this collective enterprise is that it challenges both the forms of our oppression and our uncritical acceptance of aspects of its work. Thus this coming to terms has not been an altogether comfortable journey. We, too, have had to recognise our own resentment of women for whom pregnancy is straightforward, just as we have had to acknowledge a need to embrace those women who have chosen abortion. Some of us were initially resistant to those ideas. Then we began to see that this resistance stemmed from a socially constructed division between women, one which is perceived as natural. This makes some women – those who miscarry – worthy of compassion, and others –who have a termination –deserving of blame. Those competitive relations are constructed from the identical polarities of inno-cence and guilt which form one of the major organizing principles of patri-archal control. (This can also be seen in the different kinds of treatment meted out to women who have been raped, according to how much 'to blame' they are for the assault.)[20]

The logical conclusion to this reasoning is that a woman can never be held accountable for her freely chosen decisions. They can only ever be right, worthy of compassion. But the major difference between freely chosen termination and a miscarriage or ectopic pregnancy is that one is *chosen*. It is particularly offensive to compare the experience of raped women with that of women freely choosing abortion. Contrary to male mythology, rape is never chosen. Unlike raped women, Lesley Saunders and women like her exercised a choice. They must be aware that not all choices are laudable. There is much double-think in the language and terms used in the abortion debate. To describe oneself as pro-choice particularly when one is not personally in favour of abortion but would allow others to exercise that 'right' seems the ultimate in hypocrisy. Ambivalence about abortion generally stems from what Naomi Wolf calls 'that decision, which I can't help thinking is one about life and death.'[21] Yet Naomi declares herself firmly to be pro-choice. What other life-and-death decisions would she be pro-choice about? Nuclear weapons: 'I personally do not support the use of nuclear weapons but of course I absolutely support the right of my Government to choose to deploy them as they see fit.' The burning of Asian brides who do not meet the expectations of the groom's family in relation to dowry: 'I personally deplore the tradition and would never burn a bride myself, but I support the right of the groom's family to do so, and I will march in support of that right.'

But while we are on the subject of choice, let us examine the reasons reported by the organization Open Line Counselling, for seeking abortion: Younger women feeling unprepared for a child, particularly where family and social support is unlikely or insufficient; anxiety about causing hurt to parents, espe-cially when a parent has health problems; older women being concerned about the effects of a pregnancy on a grown family, or the possibility of the foetus being disabled; instability in the relationship with the putative father, whether casual acquaintance, ex-boyfriend, or where a marriage is under stress; separated women fearful of the status of pregnancy or the effect of separation agreements; and professional women worried about the harm to their careers.[22]

All these are reasons given by women as to why they are oppressed. Abortion does not solve any of these problems, though it may temporarily relieve them. A poor woman does not cease to be poor because she aborts her child. A professional woman will not achieve equality of treatment by becoming unpregnant. Instead, it appears that, far from freedom of choice, women facing termination feel they have no choice at all — no real choice. Shouldn't feminism be working to provide women with real choices so that pregnancy does not represent disaster, personally, educationally and career-wise?

While we consent to seeing pregnancy as a curse, a life-destroying event, we facilitate society to go on acting as if this were true, instead of the social construct that it really is. Adrienne Rich and writers like her acknowledge, 'Abortion is violence; a desperate violence inflicted on a woman, first of all upon herself.'[23] Yet they still endorse the right to choose. Rich advocates the destruction of the patriarchal institution of motherhood without once ever suggesting a viable alternative.

If choice is to be real choice, what about full information? What about simple facts like 'The foetus in your womb has had a heartbeat for weeks and we can detect brain activity,' or ' you may have an increased risk of cervical incompetence and miscarriage as a result of this operation,'[24] or to a teenager, 'Your age group is most likely to suffer regret and depression as a result of this choice.'[25]

There is a concerted move in feminist circles against the technologicalization of birth and fertility. Renate Klein condemns the 'ultimate colonization' — invasive and dangerous reproductive and genetic engineering. She condemns our 'ableist' society for only sanctioning the birth of genetically 'normal' children, female foeticide, surrogacy and embryo experimentation — and then goes on to applaud 'safe, compassionate abortion'.[26] Why doesn't Klein understand just how much abortion, too, is a tool of technological and male control?

Seeing the promotion of abortion as a central tenet of feminism alienates many women, and worse, shows that women have internalized the worst excesses of male oppression. Feminism must re-evaluate its whole attitude to motherhood and reproduction. As the pro-choice author Maureen Freely writes:

> Our feminist canon tells us that an unplanned, unintended, unwanted or ill-timed baby is likely to 'ruin' a mother's life. Any woman who has gone on to give birth to one of the above in spite of these warnings can tell you, actually, it's not the baby who ruins your life. It's everyone else.[27]

She then runs through an amusing but very real litany of those people from the employer who sacks you during maternity leave to the shop door which refuses to admit a double buggy, and continues, in even more biting mode:

> Having exposed the self-serving lies of patriarchal elites, you can't help wondering about the feminist elite. What are its self-serving lies? Just how democratic and pluralistic is it? How many women can it claim to speak for?[28]

My answer to that would be; a great many more, if it were willing to admit that its emphasis on abortion has been an abuse against justice and a disaster for real choice for women.

NOTES

1 Delmar, R., 'What is Feminism?' in Mitchell, J. and Oakley, A. (eds.), *What Is Feminism?* (Blackwell Press, Oxford, 1986), 9.
2 Schneiders, S., *Beyond Patching* (Paulist Press, New York, 1991), 18–25.
3 Op cit., Delmar, 9.
4 Ruzek, S., 'Feminist Visions of Health: An International Perspective', op. cit., Mitchell and Oakley, 194.
5 Riddick, R., 'Towards a Feminist Morality of Choice' in Smith, A. (ed.), *The Abortion Papers – Ireland* (Attic Press, Dublin, 1992), 193.
6 Delmar, 8.
7 Freire, P., *Pedagogy of the Oppressed* (Penguin Books, London, 1972), 22.
8 Op. cit., Schneider, 22.
9 Tribe, L., *Abortion; The Clash of Absolutes* (Norton, New York, 1972) quoted in Suess, J.K., 'The Natural Environment of the Female Body and its Fertility' in; *Studies in Pro-Life Feminism* vol. 1, no. 1 (1995), 55.
10 Freire, op cit., 22.
11 de Beauvoir, S., *The Second Sex* (Penguin Books, London, 1972), 16.
12 Barry, K., *The Prostitution of Sexuality* (New York University Press, New York and London, 1995), 24.
13 Gilligan, C., *In a Different Voice* (Harvard University Press, Cambridge and London, 1982).
14 Op. cit., Barry, 25.
15 Barry, 24.
16 Nilson, L., *The Everday Miracle: A Child Is Born* (Allen Lane, London, 1967).
17 Barry, 69.
18 Op. cit., Riddick, 69.
19 Lesley Saunders quoted in Hey, Itzin, Saunders and Speakman (eds.), *Hidden Loss and Ectopic Pregnancy* (Women's Press, London, 1989), 10–14.
20 Ibid., 52.
21 Wolf, N., *Fire with Fire* (Chatto and Windus, London 1993), 142.
22 Riddick, 189.
23 Rich, A., *Of Woman Born* (Virago, London, 1984), 269.
24 From *Making An Informed Decision about Your Pregnancy* (Pamphlet) Pregnancy Resource Centre, Michigan, 1988.
25 Wallerstein, J.S., et al., quoted by De Veber, Parthum, Chisholm and Kiss in Gentles, I., (ed.), *A Time to Choose Life* (Stoddart, Toronto, 1990), 91.
26 Klein, R., *The Ultimate Colonization: Reproduction and Genetic Engineering* (Attic Press, Dublin, 1990).
27 Freely, M., *What about Us? An Open Letter to the Mothers Feminism Forgot* (Bloomsbury, London, 1995), 16.
28 Ibid., 52.

3

Abortion, Economics and Women's Sexuality

DIANA E. FORREST

Sexuality is a part of life. Though sexual behaviour may be seen as an escape or diversion from everyday life, and sexual morality may be seen as different from other morality, in fact it is all connected. A rich man, for example, using a sex worker's services, may see this as light relief from his usual occupation of accumulating money and power. But it is that money and power, and the sex worker's comparative lack of those, that makes the whole transaction possible.

Pornography and prostitution are sometimes recognized for what they are; sex-money exchanges. But in modern Britain love and marriage are viewed quite differently. We are no longer in the age of Jane Austen, who listed her characters' incomes in her novels. All the same, can we be sure that people marrying today never care about each other's incomes? Sexuality is affected by social and economic conditions. One example of this is women's position under patriarchy.

PATRIARCHY AND THE WOMAN AS WOMB

The word 'patriarchy' is sometimes used to mean simply 'male domination', but it has a more specific meaning. A patriarch is the male leader of a family, clan or tribe, related genetically to the people he leads, and his position is often hereditary. Children, especially sons, are therefore important to him, and to other men in such a society. A rich or powerful man may pass on property or a title to his sons. Even a poor man may pass on a name and a trade. In Britain, patriarchy is now much less common, but the Royal family (where females can succeed to the throne but males are given preference) and other titled people remain examples.

Patriarchy affects women at several stages of their lives. First, as a less valued child. Then, as a potential exchange-piece who will marry into some other family. To keep her value she must demonstrate that she is 'pure', and dispel all suspicion that she will ever mate or breed out of turn. This means that her family will control her behaviour until marriage, and her husband and his family will do so after. In marriage, she must be fertile, preferably producing sons.

Women have attacked different aspects of patriarchy in various campaigns. Women's powerlessness was tackled by winning them the vote: their ignorance by education: their seclusion in the family by getting them into employment: and their walking womb role through birth control. What effects did these campaigns have on British women's lives and sexuality? Did they get rid of patriarchy? If they did not, what did?

POLITICAL AND ECONOMIC CHANGES FOR WOMEN

Women's most important gain was the vote. Considering that women, unlike other excluded groups, make up half the population, more might have been expected from this. Yet, while some legislation benefiting women has been passed, the Houses of Commons and Lords remain male-dominated. Now that both main parties address their policies to taxpayers and not to poor people, it is becoming likely that women's interests will be less reflected in parliament.

Another struggle has been for women's education. This has succeeded so well that some people are now worried that boys are being overtaken by girls. This higher achievement, however, has not been reflected in women's employment and promotion prospects. The struggle for employment was mainly about getting women into formerly exclusively male professions. There was nothing new about poor women being employed, often as servants. Many professions are still mainly male. So is management: in 1993 only one third of managers and administrators in Britain were women. Women's hourly payments were less than four-fifths of men's.[1] Some cases of unequal pay can now be challenged legally: but it would take something as radical as a national minimum wage to make a real difference to low-paid women.

A policy of home ownership has excluded many women: and there is also a shortage of 'social' (lower rent) housing. Women therefore have an economic deterrent from living independently: yet this was what was once hoped for from women's employment. In fact, many women in employment are married or in relationships. Fewer men now earn a 'family' wage to 'keep' a non-employed wife and children: 'Most married women who work have employed partners, hence the growing divide between two-earner and no-earner households.'[2]

Yet this country is supposed to be rich, and getting richer. Some people really are rich, hence this growing gap between rich and poor. Partly, this gap is due to the way State relief of poverty is structured. While there is a safety net for most people, this net is constructed so that your feet get stuck in the mesh. There is a 'taper' on housing benefit that, together with income tax, removes most of any extra earnings.[3] Income support for unemployed people takes away any earnings over a small amount, with no allowance for work expenses. The poverty gap may not be crossed step by step, only by one giant leap.

Having children tends to put people into poverty, whether they are single or married. A couple is twice as likely to be impoverished (in the sense of having only 50% of average income after housing costs) when they have children. Single people are two and a half times as likely to be poor when they have children.[4]

The single mother living on benefit has become a hate figure for some. The old accusation of sexual immorality has now been replaced by two new accusations: That she has obtained a home and income without being in paid employment, and that she is 'married to the state' and free from the demands of a relationship with a man. The first accusation does not imply brilliant rewards for entering employment, nor does the second accusation say much for the performance of men as husbands and fathers. Do these people really believe that life on benefit, looking after a child alone in whatever is left of 'social' housing after the best bits have been sold, is the best option for a young woman? if so, they might consider what this says about young women's life chances generally.

Women who reach the top tend to be single and childless. But many women are economically better off with a partner or husband. A woman whose partner does not want a child may be faced with an economic double whammy if she decides to have one all the same, or has an unplanned child she plans to keep. First, she may be thrown out of coupledom: second, she has to bear the cost of raising a child. The result may be that she ends up on the wrong side of the poverty-riches gap. The Child Support Agency will probably be of little help because their priority is taking cash away from absent parents, not giving it to the parents with the children.

SOCIAL AND SEXUAL CHANGES FOR WOMEN: BIRTH CONTROL AND 'PERMISSIVENESS'

The birth control campaign in Britain was associated with a change in sexual behaviour—the 'Pill' and 'permissiveness'. By the 'Pill' is meant the various birth control pills. Ordinary pills that just cure diseases don't get capital letters. Was it the Pill that finally made permissiveness possible? Did permissiveness benefit women?

Some women benefitted. Those who wanted to have sex outside marriage, or who wanted to end bad marriages. There is now more openness about and acceptance of lesbianism (though there is still a long way to go). In general, there was a feeling that sex was natural and good and should not be treated as a dirty secret. However, children and their maintenance were overlooked. Even though single and divorced mothers face less stigma now, they may still be in poverty: and not all divorced women want to be divorced. And the idea of natural, good sex has not stopped pornography or prostitution. Nor has it stopped rape.

There is a viewpoint that permissiveness reflects a male desire for sex while traditional marriage reflects a woman's desire for love and commitment. There are two ways of expressing this. You can criticize women for wanting marriage because they are clinging and possessive, and after a meal ticket. Or you can compliment women for wanting marriage because they are driven by higher feelings, whereas men are so coarse they only want sex. In fact, both sexes want love and sex. Men do not express ideas of love as much as women. Some may not even be aware that they too need love, until they are deprived of it. As Orbach and Eichenbaum point out, it is the unmet needs that get noticed.[5] Men's emotional vulnerability is shown by a rising young male suicide rate.[6] Women's desire for sex has not led them all to throw off their inhibitions and their clothes and join in the 'permissive' free-for-all. Sex may be a basic instinct but security is more basic still.

Early forms of birth control were aimed mainly at women subjected to repeated childbearing. Not all feminists thought that birth control was the answer. Some argued instead for a more radical demand; women's right to refuse sex, even in marriage. But the early methods of contraception, though not 100% effective, could help those women who wanted fewer children, though not no children at all. However, permissiveness took for granted that 100% child-free sex was possible. The old methods no longer looked good enough.

The Pill was at first hailed as the answer. However, it too turned out not to be 100% effective. There were also side effects damaging to women's health, particularly poor women. Abortion, legalized for most of Britain in 1967, filled the gap. As the unborn child is a sitting target for nine months, abortion nearly always works. To some people, it looked like the solution.

Not all those who oppose abortion oppose contraception as well. Many support contraception because it does not kill. However, there is something in one of the arguments of those who oppose both; that contraception can lead to abortion. Once contraception creates the expectation, (though not the reality) of 100% child-free sex, this appears to be the norm, and getting pregnant after sex comes to look like carelessness, or at least misfortune, rather than a natural consequence. Abortion is then seen, not as an intrusion, but as restoring things to the way they ought to be.

A misleading use of language helps to grease the slippery slope from contraception to abortion. There are, in fact, three types of birth control: contraceptives which prevent conception, abortifacients which act after conception, preventing implantation (the attachment of the newly conceived embryo to the womb); and abortions, which kill the embryo or foetus after implantation but before birth. Abortifacients and abortions not only sound alike but are alike: both kill a new individual rather than ovum or sperm. However, there is a tendency to call abortifacients – or methods that may act as either abortifacient or contraceptive –contraception. A morning-after pill cannot always be contraceptive, because conception may already have happened, but, nevertheless, it is referred to as such. Women are being misled. If abortifacients are made to look like contraception, and abortions really are like abortifacients, the result is that abortions will look more like contraception.

The old-fashioned mother's answer to 'Mother, may I go and swim?' was,

Yes, my darling daughter.
Hang your clothes on a hickory limb
And don't go near the water.

Permissiveness tells the daughter that she may go right into the water — only she mustn't get wet. The modern disaster is not the loss of virginity, but getting pregnant. Why is this so? Why are some women led into a trap where they have sex that they might otherwise have opted out of, believing themselves to be safe from pregnancy, and end up having abortions? There is more to this than misinformation about birth control, though that plays a part. Of course, as we have seen, pregnancy can be an economic disaster — but *why* should it be one?

PATRIARCHS: ABDICATED OR ADJUSTED?

Is patriarchy dead? In the literal sense patriarchy may be dead for most women in Britain. A male demand for continual childbearing is no longer normal. The nature of male prestige has changed. The movement of individual people makes family ties less important and changes in work techniques mean that fewer skills are worth passing on to the next generation. A son often does not live in the same town as his father or do the same job. A father may still be proud of his son's success, but money and status contribute more to his own prestige. These days, women can help male prestige more by adding their earnings to their husband's and helping his career than they can by bearing and raising children. The economic cost of childbearing may seem too high to one or both partners.

Economics will not have the same effect on everybody. Some people will want a child not because of prestige but so that they can love, accept and get to know him or her. Some people will not want a child at all. However, a deterrent effect has already shown up. According to a recent Family Policy Studies Centre report, one young woman in five does not have children, compared with only one in ten in her mother's generation.[7]

Permissiveness represents the death of patriarchy, but not the death of male domination. Male domination has merely changed its nature. More people should have asked what 'permissiveness' really meant — who was permitted to do what. The lack of concern for children and mothers should have provided a clue. Permissiveness is just men giving each other permission to treat women differently and make different demands on them. If there is less call for child-bearing then fewer women need to be 'pure' and more can be available for sex with men: child-free sex, of course. This change of demands has sometimes been mistaken for sexual liberation, but explains why pornography, prostitution and rape continue: they are symptoms of continuing male domination.

It also explains why technical fixes like employment and birth control failed to deliver as much as women hoped. They were designed to counteract patriarchy, but in the present situation, they often operate to adjust women to conform to men's new demands. Some women have spotted a catch. Sheila Jeffreys concludes that power differences between men and women influence heterosexual relationships, and that, for example, a male cruising lifestyle does not work for women because they do not have the power to carry it through.[8]

Many feminists recognize pornography and prostitution as aspects of male oppression. Two out of three is not bad. The following are true of pornography, or prostitution – and also of abortion:

1   They result from sexual desire, detached from respect for persons.

2   People may be driven to each by poverty, while in contrast, those maintaining the practices can make large profits.

3   Each is not defended as good in itself, only as a 'choice'.

4   Each is also defended by the argument that it is ineradicable, so might as well be legalized as a damage limitation exercise.

5   All the same, each can damage health, even if legal isn't it time the penny dropped?

MARKET FORCES AND FEMINISM

Of course, not everyone recognizes that women are still being oppressed post-patriarchy. Some people look on the bright side of a changing economics and society. 'Bored with politics? Tired of being ignored when you demand your human rights? Then get out there and compete.' This is the implication. It might be feasible if unregulated competition and human freedom were the same thing, as they are sometimes assumed to be. But have the winds of competition blown away the old prejudices? From the Equal Opportunities Commission statistics it doesn't look like it. If a company actually does hire the best people regardless of sex, race, age, sexual preference or disability, they may gain a competitive advantage. But that doesn't say they have to. Perhaps they would rather keep their prejudices and pay the price. And, if women in a position to compete still have problems, what about the losers?

They get 'choices'. The word 'choice' tends not to precede good news. In work, it can mean bad pay and conditions. Sometimes it even means prostitution. Unregulated competition and freedom are not the same thing, or even alike. They might be if we were in a wilderness where everyone could go out with a few tools, take as much land as they needed, and carve out a living for themselves. People who try to live in this way are now hounded from place to place and condemned. The alternative is to conform and be subject to the will of landlords, employers and the State, unless you acquire enough money to buy yourself free, which will never happen for many people. Capitalist 'freedom' is an illusion for many people, just as sexual 'freedom' is an illusion for many women.

THE WELFARE COST OF ECONOMICS

Many of the technical fixes that have so far failed to make women equal are conditional: 'You can be equal once you are . . .' (educated; employed; child-free). When society changed, these became less ways of liberating women then of ways of adjusting them to the new demands of a male dominated society.

Rather than deciding what an equal woman ought to be like and trying to fit real women to this image, we need to struggle for unconditional equality if equality is what we want. Nor should we proclaim that women are kinder, gentler, nicer human beings than men and therefore deserve to be equal. We must demand equality because women are human beings.

But unborn children are human beings too. It has not helped women's cause to assert how superior they are to unborn children. The tactic of oppressed people fighting each other is a poor one. It implies that some oppression is acceptable. It also diverts energy away from the real oppressors. The rights of women and unborn children must be defended together. At the same time, many of those who oppose abortion need to take on board the pro-choice criticism that, though they defend the lives of children not yet born, they are not concerned enough about how those children will continue to survive after birth.

Radical political changes need economic changes too. At present, people serve economic goals not so much because they see the point of them but in order that, in return, they may be allowed to survive. If human rights to life and equality really matter, then we must stand economics on its head. It must be redesigned to serve human survival first.

HOW IT COULD BE

In a society where each human being's survival and well-being was of the first importance, child care would be important too, rather than an annoying distraction from the goals of the economy. It would be seen as real work, as would looking after old and incapacitated people. This is not a call for women to get back in the home and save the world. Nothing says that child care should only be done by women, nor does it have to be done only in the home. Nor does that home have to be the home of a nuclear family.

The traditional nuclear family could still survive, but only if it works for all its members. Working for the person or persons whose opinions are considered to matter will no longer be good enough. There are many other kinds of families in which children might be brought up. And single people without children could be part of families also.

There would be less hierarchy and control over other people. Work and home would be less rigidly separated and people would have more control over their time. Of course, I am not prescribing an instant utopia. There would still be much work that had to be done, with particular urgency, since so much work done now is for wasteful and destructive purposes. Those who had once held power would have to learn how to do without it. This would mean learning to relate to people without the short cuts and evasions that power makes possible. Those who had been powerless might have problems too: rigidity caused by oppression can feel like a support.

And there could still be losers in this new society: only, because of the different priorities, they would no longer be written off as unimportant: their welfare and empowerment would be important. It would not be a society without pain. But there would be less pain of adjusting to oppression and more growing pains.

For the first time men and women might enter sexual relationships on equal terms and without oppressive expectations or implicit threats. Any concern to prevent conception would be shared. The expression of male power would no longer infect sex. People might realize that other forms of sex can be as important as penetration, and other forms of sensuality can be as important as sex. Pleasures like massage and dancing would be valued more in their own right, for example. But, before we can have sexuality as if women mattered, we must have economics as if people mattered.

NOTES

1 *Some Facts about Women* (Equal Opportunities Commission, London 1994).
2 'Working Women Hold the Key to Children's Future', *The Guardian*, 5 September 1994.
3 *Housing Rights – a Shelter Guide – Housing Benefit* (Shelter, London, 1993).
4 Child Poverty Action Group, Key Poverty Statistics, October 1994.
5 Eichenbaum, L., and Orbach, S., *What Do Women Want?* (Fontana, London, 1994), 77
6 'Giving up on Life', *The Guardian*, 3 December 1994.
7 'Motherhood Going out of Fashion for Young Women', *Daily Telegraph*, 10 April 1996.
8 Jeffreys, S., *Anticlimax* (Women's Press, London, 1990).

Socialism and Abortion

ANN FARMER

At home, we never discussed religion, it was always politics. When I was born, when I grew up, there was still a thing called class consciousness. People remembered how bad things had been under the Tories, how much they owed to Labour. To my: 'Are we rich or are we poor?' my mother would reply: 'We're not rich and we're not poor.' To her, who had known poverty, this was true. But in the Fifties, with five children to bring up on one man's wage, we were poorer than many. However, this was not a cause of shame to someone with class consciousness. It was the Capitalist system to blame, big business and the Tories. Through my mother and father, I learned working-class history. Their childhood stories were my political education.

My maternal grandmother entered 'service' at the age of twelve, but soon left —apparently unable to touch her forelock convincingly enough. At eighteen, she married a glass-blower in the Balls Pond Road. He had a trade, so they were better off than many, but my mother remembers going with her sister to pawn the Sunday suits on Monday morning, giving an assumed name, and coming home 'the long way' in case anyone recognized them. Grandma had an expression: 'Stock's as good as money' — in other words, if you haven't got material things, you've still got your children. What she longed for was not fewer children, but somewhere decent to bring up the ones she had. She was overjoyed when she was allocated one of the first LCC flats on a Hackney estate which would probably now be called run-down. To her, it was heaven. No more late-night trips around the bedroom with a candle, to catch the bugs emerging from the walls. No more trips to the public baths, soap and towel in hand.

My father came from what they now call a single-parent home. Grandad got going when the going got tough – which it did, quite often. Dad remembers vividly standing in front of Hackney Workhouse having walked miles from Shoreditch, only for his mother to be told that she was in the wrong Parish. In true Malthusian tradition —the sexes were segregated to prevent breeding—Dad was separated from his mother and his little sisters, one of whom died in that workhouse. Later, he was rescued from Grandad, who was using him as an unpaid electrical assistant, letting him sleep on two wooden chairs at night, and sent to a succession of children's homes with his brothers. Throughout, he 'looked out' for his little brother, often taking punishments for him. They ended up in a farm orphanage in Yorkshire, where Dad was a ploughboy and slept over the stables. He was saved from being sent to Canada with a group of 'orphans' when Grandma turned up to claim him.

What did this teach me about socialism? That the Capitalist system bears down on the weakest. And the weakest in the chain is the child. What did it teach me about feminism? That without rights, women are always too vulnerable. Their role as mothers makes them vulnerable. They can never up and leave when the fancy takes them. And also that rights are a positive thing – the right to vote, to equal pay, to a pension. Not the negative rights of exploiting or oppressing others. In the end, socialism and feminism must come together in co-operation, because two halves of the human race can only work if they work together.

Where does abortion fit in? When I was a child, I read the *Daily Herald* from cover to cover. I listened to the politics on the telly. I don't remember abortion being an issue. This is not to say that it was not debated in loftier circles than a terraced council house in Essex. The Sixties was a time of great optimism, of fun, especially for young people. A sense of hope prevailed, quite unknown to today's youngsters. We had a Labour Government, building Council houses, rooting for British industry, working for more equality in education.

But, in a succession of dead-end jobs, I discovered the 'glass ceiling' of class discrimination, that invisible barrier that excludes anyone with talent but no further education from progressing upward. There was also an age-gap in the female workforce: very young girls, and unqualified older women, with management posts taken by indifferent men. I came up against a double discrimination of class and sex. Without a union, workers, especially women, were exploited. But union meetings were held in the evening, when married women would be rushing home to start the 'second shift'. They would struggle back from their lunchbreak laden with shopping, while men seemed to carry nothing heavier than a newspaper. Equality of opportunity for women seemed to involve extending the number of tasks they could perform without collapsing.

Still, abortion never seemed to figure as an issue for ordinary women in the seventies, even when the Corrie Bill was being hotly debated in Parliament. In my young socialist days, the hot topic was Northern Ireland. People nearly came to blows over the rights and wrongs of military intervention. A Labour Government had sent in the troops – albeit as a calming and protective measure – but things were getting out of hand. To some, violence could never be a solution. To others, it was a legitimate means to an end.

I joined the Labour Party in 1979. Margaret Thatcher had just been elected, I was expecting my first baby, and was full of foreboding. Many women had voted Conservative because Mrs Thatcher 'was a woman'. In the years to come, I felt she gave womanhood a bad name – especially women in power. I was disappointed that the feminists gave her such an easy ride. After all, we had always believed that if women could come to power, everything would be better. Well, they did, but it wasn't. Still, abortion was not Big News in the Labour Party. The bone of contention was the European Community. Later, we were tearing ourselves apart over unilateral disarmament. There were so many opinions on these and other issues, that it seemed quite normal to have a number of opinions on something like abortion.

But times change. The left-wing press, which at one time gave free rein to all views, changed. *Militant, Tribune, Socialist Worker*, all adopted pro-abortion policies. For a while they would print a pro-life view – especially if it came from a man – but gradually, even that avenue closed. I am eternally grateful that *Labour Weekly*, in its final issue in 1987, gave me space to put the pro-life case during the Alton Bill.

Growing up a socialist, I always had the strange idea that things could only get better; but how quickly, and easily the achievements of various Labour administrations could be wiped out by a determined right-wing government! Even the gains made in women's equality could back-fire, giving us equality – but at a price. Yet, despite the loss of benefits under the Tories, one 'advance' for women remains untouched. We still have abortion.

ABORTION AS A DISINCENTIVE TO SOCIAL REFORM

Most revolutions have had a common feature. They endeavour to give equality to women, perhaps because revolutions need women's help to succeed. Communist Russia was a beacon to the Left in the Twenties and Thirties. Its oppressive nature ignored, we saw only what we wanted to see. As with most violent revolutions, the oppression continued, under a different guise, but with a loftier purpose. Women had access to abortion. But they were also expected to do heavy manual labour, look after the house, and queue for hours for food. Abortion gave them the opportunity to become surrogate men – but without the leisure. If the flat was too small, if they had to work, if their husband would not help with the chores, they could still have abortion. Post-Communism, they still have these opportunities, plus the good old Capitalist escape routes of beauty queen or prostitute.

Those who say that abortion is a sad, but rare choice, need only look to Russia, with four million conducted every year,[1] to realize that abortion can become a way of life. Not that women are unaffected by abortion. But where society accepts abortion, human life becomes cheapened, and it is harder for women to argue for maternal rights, better maternity provision, family benefits. Motherhood is seen as an optional extra, a kind of female aberration, rather than something natural and normal. It seems strange that, in this country, a Labour Government, which introduced the welfare state, legalized abortion, just when motherhood could be experienced without fear of extreme financial hardship. Were the politicians counting the cost to the nation of too many poor babies? Writing on the patriarchal state, Drude Dahlerup discusses the view that 'free abortion came at the time it did because women's stable labour force was needed by the employers', but goes on to question: 'If this is so, why do some countries get free abortion in times of economic crises and massive unemployment?'[2] The answer is obvious – to pro-life feminists at any rate – it is because, in a welfare state, babies cost the state money! Recently, government ministers criticized single mothers for draining the welfare state. It is not unusual nowadays for single mothers to find themselves allocated a flat without any furniture, or even a bed to sleep on. Any special needs must be met from loans, which will not be granted if they are too poor to pay them back. During the debate on single mothers, the A-word was conspicuous by its absence. Nobody actually said publicly to single pregnant women, have an abortion. But a flat, a cot, or a pram, cannot be obtained with two doctors' signatures. Abortion has become the official, if unnamed, safety-valve for social reform for women.

SOCIALIST WOMEN AND ABORTION

'But rich women have always had access to abortion.' If I had five new pence for every time I'd heard that one, I'd be a rich woman myself by now. The feeling of injustice, that rich people have something which the rest have been denied, is constantly exploited to justify abortion. But should we be emulating rich women? Should we be sending our children away to school, parking them with nannies, only seeing them during the holidays? Can I be the only woman who feels horror at the thought of sending her children away 'for their own benefit'? Foreigners think it strange that the English upper classes send their children away but keep their dogs at home. It appals me that socialist women might think this an enviable state of affairs.

Other socialist women justify abortion for health reasons. Understandably, they fear that de-legalization of abortion will lead to a return to the back-street. But what led women to illegal abortion? Deplorable social conditions, lack of ante-natal and maternity care, benefits and accommodation, lack of income. Desperate women, desperate remedies. But back-street abortion harks back further than 1967, to the Thirties, or beyond. Abortion deaths, with all female deaths, have continued a steady decline since the beginning of this century.[3] The founders of the Labour Party did not demand legal abortion to combat female poverty or illegal abortion. They demanded social justice. Abortion is not a remedy for poverty. It never has been. It cannot do away with social deprivation. It can only kill.

Why is it that what was clear to our foremothers, we fail to see? The Channel 4 programme 'Desperate Choices', showed US women 'choosing' abortion owing to material poverty and relationship difficulties, feeling they had no choice. If all poor pregnant women were adequately provided for, very few would 'choose' abortion. What then would become of those better-off women who want legal abortion in case they need it themselves? Poor women have been sacrificed to the political interests of middle-class women. The National Abortion Campaign have stated that the only qualification for abortion is that the woman concerned wants it.[4] If this were followed through, it would entail a massive expansion of abortion facilities. Lack of doctor's involvement would bring increased health risks. There would be no time limit, meaning abortion up to birth on demand (already allowed for disabled fetuses since the Embryology Act of 1991). The wish to protect life, diminished since 1967, would wither completely. (NB One reason proposed for abortion is the elimination of 'unwanted' children. The rate of death of children caused by battering in the Irish Republic and Northern Ireland is 0.0 – the figures are too low to be measured. In comparison, an NSPCC 'league table' of child murders among the world's most developed nations lists England and Wales as the fourth highest, with most infants killed aged less than one year.[5] Ireland also has a lower maternal mortality rate than the UK, despite having a higher birthrate.)[6]

Since the unborn child is not worthy of respect, why respect the born child? Or her mother? Ante-natal care, premature baby care, foetal medicine and infertility treatment would be under even greater pressure in a society which no longer cares.

PRO-CHOICE – NO CHOICE?

Socialist feminists have an ambivalent attitude to abortion. It is a terrible decision which no woman undergoes lightly – but on the other hand, there are no after-effects, and it's no big deal.

They ignore basic socialist concerns such as maternal poverty, coercion and the human rights of the unborn child. When they speak of the most important issues for women, they emphasize child care and equality in the work-place. But when a restrictive Bill is under debate in Parliament, suddenly we can't exist without abortion, the cornerstone of human rights. When it comes to hot topics, there are none hotter than abortion, and none of which its advocates know so little. It worries me that any woman might knowingly champion such a barbarous procedure.

Abortion is perceived as a woman's issue, one on which it is necessary only to vote in the correct way. Since the 1985 Labour Party Conference resolution on restricting Labour MPs' conscience vote on abortion legislation, it has been claimed that the defence of the 1967 Abortion Act is Party policy. While no such bill has ever been 'whipped', and we have been assured that MPs are indeed free to vote in conscience,[7] this resolution has had appalling results. The Labour Party has become known as the Party that orders its MPs' consciences. It has become harder for pro-life views to be expressed. Pro-life socialists are subjected to harrassment and discrimination.[8] It will be harder for Parliamentary hopefuls to be selected if they oppose abortion. Constituencies where Labour voters might object to a pro-abortion Labour MP will have no choice. Labour will become known as the Party which will not allow dissent on a difficult moral issue. To say that we should simply acknowledge the right of women to choose abortion, is akin to saying that we should acknowledge that people should be hanged if an individual judge favours it.

Emily's List was launched in Britain to help Labour woment into Parliament, its only proviso that applicants be 'pro-choice'.[9] Emily's List has exposed the paranoid (no other word will do, since we are a tiny minority) attitude of some socialist women to pro-life socialist women. It must be our arguments which they fear, especially when they are women's arguments, as they prefer to portray abortion as a man versus woman issue. They have spent so long agreeing among themselves, that when confronted with a different view, they resort to anger instead of reasoned argument. I believe Emily's List is purely a way of getting pro-abortion Labour women into Parliament. The British 1967 Act has become elevated to icon status. Most believe it to be a triumph of feminism, when it resulted from the thalidomide tragedy, combined with a fear of over-population, fought for by a small unrepresentative pressure group, and granted by a patrician liberal government.[10]

FALSE EQUALITY?

Feminist arguments for abortion are driven by injustice against women. But they cannot justify the oppression of weaker members of society. Because I am oppressed by my boss, does not mean I have the right to oppress my children. Because millions of women were burned at the stake as witches does not justify the disposal of unborn human life with methods just as cruel and painful.

Feminists, drawing attention to the wrongs of men, fail to criticize their role in the abortion process. If women were emotionally or physically blackmailed into prostitution, or shoplifting, there would be a feminist outcry. Why, then, the silence about male complicity in abortion? Why always present it as a simple choice for women? Is it because they fear admission of the negative aspects will lead to people questioning abortion itself? Abortion cannot produce equality – only the chance to compete with men on their (childless) terms, and only temporarily. Once a woman has children (if her fertility has not been ruined by abortion), she will have to accommodate herself to the system, instead of the system accommodating the perfectly natural sequence of pregnancy, birth and child care. Ironically, Emily campaigners have missed the point. Parliament allows women to change themselves and fit in by becoming un-pregnant (by abortion), but will not reform its own working practices to become more woman-friendly. Men need not change, but women must.

THE SOCIALIST MOVEMENT AND ABORTION

Even history is distorted to 'show' that the Labour Party has always been pro-abortion.[11] If the Labour pioneers had promised the working classes the right to dispose of their children, would we ever have been elected? It is no coincidence that we have been rejected by the electorate consistently since 1979. Once you silence your conscience on one injustice, you lose the courage of your convictions. When Marie Stopes opened her first birth control clinic in Holloway, London, in 1921, she never considered whether women wanted housing, clothes and shoes for their children, a living wage for their husbands and security in old age. Marie Stopes was neither socialist nor feminist, yet has become a heroine of both movements. Why? What possible electoral advantage is there in limiting the number of working class people? Birth control, whether before or after conception, has been the response of the middle to the working classes since Malthus. The tragedy is, we've bought it. It shows in the reluctance to speak positively of the family; with references to the 'burden of child care'. Abortion has distorted attitudes on many issues. Single mother's rights to housing were not championed — would it have lessened the demand for abortion if all single mothers were decently provided for? Why have we not raised a stink over profits from abortion and fertility treatment? What about the health risks from abortion, including the chemical RU486? Abortion and child care are twin preoccupations of Labour policy — two sides of the same coin, or guilty conscience? Or are they merely two ways of ensuring equality for women by removing the necessity to care for children?

Historically, little is known of whether prominent Labour leaders were 'pro' or 'anti' abortion. Were they anti-women? Or was it that being anti-abortion was the norm and not, as it now is, the mark of an endangered species? Then, abortion was not striven for like some marvellous benefit. It was seen, at best, as the act of a desperate woman. Why, with such vast improvements in social conditions, are so many women still desperate?

HEALTH CARE ECONOMICS

While totalitarian regimes decide who should live and who should die, in democratic states, no such mandates are issued. However, financial conditions are created, to the disadvantage of the neediest, which drive them to make unpalatable 'choices'. The state stands aside from controversial matters such as abortion.[12] But the grounds are elastic enough to permit abortion for any reason.[13] Even distress at pregnancy is taken as a good enough reason. And financial problems constitute a reason for distress.

Now that the wealthy take financial responsibility (through their taxes and rates) for poor children, abortion is seen as a sensible 'option' for any woman who has not the means to bring up a child. Of course, some continue to have children they cannot 'afford'. Single mothers are to be 'helped back to work' – it being known that working women have fewer children. There is no more need for incarceration of unmarried mothers to stop them 'breeding', or the segregation of the workhouse. The 'right to choose' combined with low-paid work and lack of childcare takes care of everything. The economics of health care started with the legalization of abortion.[14] Endless resources are pumped into the detection of disability in the womb, compared to actually helping disabled people and their families to lead better lives.[15] Now, attention has turned to brain-injured patients, newborn disabled infants, premature babies, and children who need expensive treatment. 'Quality of life' criteria is increasingly applied to all sorts of people. Some will no doubt argue that women should be allowed to abort girls because of gender prejudice, and black women to abort because of racial prejudice.

In a time of shrinking opportunities for young people, some would call it madness to bring another child into the world. It might be seen as kind to kill an unborn child to spare it the misery of growing up with a poor education, unemployment, and no hope – to spare it, in short, from being working class. There is no need for a modern democratic state to decree who shall live and who shall die. But when the present generation grow old, and the shrinking number of young people begin to regard us with horror, assess our 'quality of life', and the financial drain on their purse, will the state allow them the choice of euthanasia for their unwanted parents? When people can be killed with kindness, who needs dictators?

ABORTION AND CONSUMERISM

The language of choice appeals to our helplessness in the face of immutable forces, purporting to give back some of the human dignity taken from us by an inhuman economic system. We are persuaded that we preside over our own fate. It particularly appeals to young people desiring freedom. But who allows us to choose? An unplanned pregnancy can come like a bolt from the blue, in an age accustomed to making choices. We chose contraception, we chose not to get pregnant. But nobody told us that contraceptives don't always work, and we are pregnant against our will. It seems the ultimate reminder of our helplessness in the hands of fate. But in the modern age, where choice has become a modern religion, there is always abortion. No one contemplates it as a positive choice. It is there, at the margins of our consciousness, not relevant to our situation, until our situation changes, and abortion becomes a possibility.

Modern 'pro-choice' feminists do not claim to be for abortion, but for a woman's right to choose abortion if she so wishes. It is presented, not as a good thing, but to allow women not to be pregnant against their will. The right to choose is fought for, and vehemently defended against attack. But what are we choosing? Not soap powder, baked beans, hairspray – or even a house or a job. We are choosing between human life, and human death. How easily this simple fact can be overlooked, when we employ the language of choice, freedom and rights.

Because modern feminism has marginalized the pro-life feminist view, it is easy to ignore the human life argument. There are feminists to put the case, but it goes unheard because feminist publications and liberal journals are closed to pro-life feminism. This may seem a simple, if appalling, way of getting around the human life argument. But truth is not so easily silenced, and if its voice is denied or distorted, it will simply relocate and speak from outside the cosy consensus. The language of choice reduces human beings either to consumers or consumed. The strong and the weak. The accepted and the rejected. The qualified and the unqualified. The chosen and the not-chosen. Seeing abortion as a 'choice' has distorted our views on so many other issues: surrogate mothers; sex-selection abortion; forced abortion; population control. The hideous cracks caused by abortion must be ignored if the great god is to remain intact on its crumbling plinth. The language of choice is not relevant to abortion, capital punishment, war, hunting or any other life or death issue. But abortions are not carried out in public, or shown on the Nine O' Clock News. Abortion advocates can continue to speak of choice. Luckily for them, reality has not yet penetrated the arguments.

OPPOSITION TO ABORTION: A RIGHT-WING OBJECTIVE?

What is a feminist? There are no formal qualifications, not even that of female-hood. Men can be feminists. Feminism is fluid and adaptable, versatile and unstructured. This is a source of strength, but also a weakness, if you want to get things done. Feminists who want to get things done join political parties. Historically, they have tended to join parties of the Left because socialists have been sympathetic to suppressed sections of society. Because of its lack of structure and formality, modern feminism has evolved into a movement of words, not actions.

The strangest of role models have been claimed for feminism. Left-wing feminists have claimed Edwina Currie and Teresa Gorman, both Conservative MPs, as feminists. While feminism has included even such dubious examples as Madonna in their embrace, and even 'sex workers' are applauded as signs of a wonderfully diverse movement, the one thing that feminism does seem to agree on is that it must embrace abortion. So, when Madonna is claimed as a feminist, and Mother Teresa is put beyond the ideological pale, you can guess why.

By the same token, opponents of abortion are without hesitation termed right-wing, again, even if they have never claimed to be. Pro-abortion commentators often ascribe words or ideas to anti-abortionists which those people never used. For example, I have frequently read of anti- abortionists allegedly using the expression 'murder'. Their motives are questioned; it is not accepted that they do not like abortion and are therefore working against it. They are said to be 'specific issue antagonists', or 'disputing rights of ownership of the foetus'.[16] They are accused of having 'strange bed-fellows' because some people (who freely admit right-wing views) are also anti-abortion. No-one associates pro-abortion views with right-wing views, even when there are plenty of willing candidates.

Abortion has distorted feminism in the same way that it has distorted socialism. It has become the sacred cow which no-one dares to touch. Any other issue that connects with abortion rights is affected. So male coercion in abortion is not acknowledged. Labour policy on Northern Ireland has been soft-pedalled, because of efforts to impose the 1967 Act.[17] Feminists have been trying to get more women into Parliament – but only if they are pro-abortion. The most rampantly right-wing government of modern times was led by a woman – but Margaret Thatcher was not criticized. While restricting women's choice in a number of areas, she did not restrict their 'choice' of abortion.

If the point of feminism is to obtain justice for women, then women politicians should be working for justice for women. Abortion is certainly not justice for women, it is merely a sop to discontented women. It is the status quo. If we accept that the status quo is unjust, then why are we so strenuously supporting a device that upholds it? Instead of pursuing real justice for women, socialists have subcontracted their consciences to an unrepresentative clique of modern feminist blackmailers. Instead of delivering real justice for women, they have delivered abortion. Not only are they damaging women and children, but in the process are damaging both socialism and feminism.

NOTES

1 Four million abortions are officially registered in Russia annually, but the true figure may be much higher. According to UN figures, there are 119.6 abortions per1,000 Russian women aged 15–44 (the UK figure is 14.8).

2 Dahlerup, D., 'Confusing Concepts – Confusing Reality: a Theoretical Discussion of the Patriarchial State' in Showstack Sasson, A. (ed.), *Women and the State* (Routledge, London, 1992), 93–127.

3 The female death rate fell sharply from three per 1,000 women (aged 5–44) in 1931, to one per 1,000 from 1951 onwards. (CSO *Social Trends* 1971).

4 Letter to *Spare Rib* magazine (Dec. 1991/Jan. 1992 issue), from Leonora Lloyd and Mandy Coates of the National Abortion Campaign.

5 *Human Concern*, Summer 1994.

6 Ireland has two deaths per 100,000 women relating to pregnancy and childbirth; Britain has eight deaths per 100,000 women. (Progress of Nations, UNICEF).

7 Neil Kinnock MP, then Labour leader, commenting to *The Universe* (18 October 1985). He spoke strongly against the motion in the Labour Party National Executive Committee because

of the conscience question, and secured a majority of the NEC to vote against. The NEC advised the Conference to vote against. In a letter to the author, Tony Blair MP, then Shadow Home Secretary, stated: 'There is no official Labour position on the abortion issue. It is recognised by the Party and indeed by Parliament that this is a matter of conscience subject to a free vote.'

8 For example, at the Brighton Conference, a woman was allowed to seize the speaker's microphone and urge 'everyone' to picket the Labour Life Group fringe meeting. The meeting was besieged by protestors, who proceeded to note the names of any delegates who attempted to attend the meeting.

9 The Emily's List has attracted high-profile support. Its original sponsors included six Labour women MPs and one Labour woman MEP.

10 Simms, M. and Hindell, K., *Abortion Law Reformed* (Peter Owen, London, 1971).

11 Soloway, R., *Birth Control and the Population Question in England 1877–1930* (University of Carolina Press, Chapel Hill, London, 1982).

12 Pfeffer, N., *The Stork and the Syringe: A Political History of Reproductive Medicine* (Polity Press, London, 1993).

13 In May 1993, Mrs Sarbjit Kaur Lall obtained an abortion for her fourth child, without revealing the true reasons for her request, which was that she already had three daughters and wanted a son. She had already obtained a private diagnosis of the sex of the foetus. She died after massive internal bleeding from a perforated uterus and subsequent cardiac arrest. The case illustrates the fact that a woman's request for abortion will be treated sympathetically if (as Mrs Lall claimed) she says she cannot afford another child.

14 'The cost of caring for severely handicapped spina bifida children may well make this type of selection [pre-natal diagnosis and abortion] economically worthwhile' ('DHSS Cost Benefit Analysis', *General Practitioner*, 1 October 1976).

15 'If resources really are saved from community budgets by [ante-natal] screening (by avoiding the costs of care for people with Down's syndrome), perhaps some of the savings might be directed back to improving screening programmes themselves' (Letter to *The Independent*, 28 January 1994, from Andrew J. Dawson, senior lecturer in obstetrics, University of Wales; Tim Reynolds, consultant in chemical pathology, Burton Group of Hospitals, Staffs; and Gillian Jones, research midwife, University of Wales).

16 'Motivations of the Antifeminists', in Rowlands, R. (ed.), *Women Who Do and Women Who Don't Join the Women's Movement* (Routledge & Kegan Paul, London, 1984), 22–4.

17 Labour's Northern Ireland spokeswoman, Dr Marjorie Mowlam MP, has pledged to introduce the 1967 Abortion Act to Northern Ireland, despite the fact that a Parliamentary Bill to this effect was not able to command the support of a single Northern Irish MP (speech at Belfast University on 22 October 1995, quoted in the *Christian Democrat* December 1995). Dr Mowlam is a patron of Emily's List. Her Deputy is Tony Worthington MP, a Vice-President of Population Concern.

5

The Nature of the Foetus:
A Vegetarian Argument against
Abortion

ALI BROWNING

A PERSONAL HISTORY

I became opposed to abortion, vivisection and killing animals for meat and fur, at the age of eleven. I had always hated suffering and pain, and found abortion and animal abuse abhorrent in my young mind, not because of anything that my elders had told me, but through seeing pictures of animals in laboratories and abattoirs, and pictures of dead aborted foetuses. These images disturbed me.

I showed the pictures of the foetuses, found in one of my parents' evangelical Christian journals, to my mother, and asked why were there so many tiny, dead babies in bins. She said that abortion was a very wicked thing which happened when people had sex before marriage. Among the strict religious circles of my childhood, opposition to abortion was linked to sexual morality and a woman's duty to have children. But my problem with abortion was that it killed a human being, reinforcing the notion that some human beings have a right to ownership of other humans.

As I got older I searched for and found a lot more about abortion and animal rights. I linked them because, in both cases, a living being, unable to defend itself, is killed. Because neither foetuses nor animals can talk, it is argued that it is not wrong to eat meat or perform abortions, that neither are sentient beings. An animal is seen as 'lower' than a human, and a foetus, in our pro-abortion culture, is never viewed as having equal rights to its mother. These arguments just did not, in my view, hold water.

Problems arose for me when I discovered feminism and began to question and eventually to reject the strict religious teaching I had been reared on, discovering my own values, my own expression of spirituality. To me, the bible was full of deliberate killing and intolerance, asserting that taking a life was wrong, yet promoting the slaughter of tribes or races with different beliefs. There is also a lack of concern for unborn life in the bible. One Old Testament verse appears to say that a woman suspected of adultery could be given a bitter herb, which, if she was guilty, would cause internal damage: if innocent, she would be pregnant.[1]

Some bible scholars believe that this herb induced miscarriage[2] – Abortion, sanctioned by the religious leaders of the time? It seems no man was to be punished for committing adultery, just women and babies. Another verse states that someone causing a woman to miscarry during physical struggle was to pay money as compensation to her husband.[3] As the law of Moses demanded that the taker of a person's life should pay for that sin with their own, it seems that religious leaders did not see unborn children as equal to born humans.

I also could not understand the anti-contraception stance taken by some anti-abortionists. To me, here is a great difference between abortion and contraception. The latter does not destroy life, it prevents ovum and sperm forming a new person. Contraception may prevent the creation of life, but then so will abstinence.

I had assumed that pacifists, animal rights supporters and socialists would be against abortion. Feminists, too, would be against abortion because they would care for those persecuted and denied equal rights. I assumed they would reject the slogan 'the right to choose' because that implies that the baby is the property of its mother, not an individual, unless she decides to grant it that status. Women themselves were once viewed as the property of men, of fathers and husbands, with no individual rights.[4] I thought that feminists had seen the connection. But I was shocked to discover that the 'right-on' people I so admired as a teenager were all in favour of the right to abortion and dismissed the pro-life lobby as being religious and right-wing. To me, pro-life philosophy was no more 'religious' than anti-apartheid campaigns or those against poverty. But I was told that unless I supported abortion on demand I was not a proper feminist, but a collaborater with male oppressors, causing setbacks in the fight for women's rights.

So, at the time of the Alton Bill,[5] I became 'pro-choice' for a few months, purely because it seemed a rule I must obey if I was to call myself a feminist. I had come from a background in which I had been told that I could not be Christian unless I was a born-again, evangelical Protestant. I was used to repressing my views that I had from the heart and obeying rules so that I could fit in and not cause discord. This situation was no different.

But in the end I could not convince myself of the pro-choice argument, believing I had no right to campaign against animal abuse whilst I believed that it was acceptable for foetuses to be killed. I was weary of being told what to believe by religious edict, and would not have the feminist movement tell me what to believe either. If feminism was about liberation, then I had every right to dissent on the abortion issue. I also did not think that women could build up our liberation upon a mound of corpses, in the way that revolutions brought about by men often did.

PROPERTY

People often argue that it is acceptable to eat meat and use animals for experiments because they are the property of humans. The 'property ethic' has been and is still used to excuse much injustice and acts of cruelty and oppression. Animals are bought and sold, destroyed without question, eaten, used to entertain people, sacrificed, tortured, used and abused. There are even those who enjoy inflicting pain on vulnerable living things; children as well as animals. Owning property gives power; owning a living thing means power over that other life. Owning land means the owner can use and abuse it as they choose. In a television debate between a hunt saboteur and a pro-hunting land-owner, the irate land-owner spouted that it was his land and his right to choose what happened on it. Those words sounded familiar.

Of course, deciding what to do with your own life, destiny and body are basic human rights. Liberty is important but not absolute. The right to liberty ends where the next person's rights begin. Power and ownership breeds slavery, oppression and the notion that there is a right to kill and abuse. We do not have such a right.

The foetus, growing within the body of a woman, is valued only as part of its mother's body until the time it is born. But an examination of foetal development shows that the foetus is not a body part of its mother, but a separate human individual: it cannot be considered the property of its mother just because it needs to grow in her body.

FOETAL DEVELOPMENT

The term *foetus* in Latin means 'little one', and is used in medical science to describe a mammalian embryo during the later stages of development within the womb.[6] Each human cell normally contains 46 chromosomes, except male sperm and female ovum cells. These have 23 each. At conception one ovum and one sperm usually[7] fuse, creating a new cell with 46 chromosomes. Gender, hair and eye colour, physical characteristics and to some extent personality and intelligence are determined when this new cell is created. This cell is unique, there will never be another one quite like it. It contains genetic information from both parents and other generations from the family of the parents. When this cell divides for the first time it is known as a blastocyst, a very early human embryo. Six to eight days after ovulation the blastocyst attaches itself to the lining of the womb where it begins to grow and develop. The cell divides rapidly after fertilization. When the fertilized ovum divides for the first time one part develops into the baby; the other becomes the placenta. The placenta supplies the developing foetus with oxygen and nutrition during pregnancy, and gets rid of waste products.

This new being is not like any other cell in the human body. It has been created from the cells of the mother and father, but unlike other cells in the body it belongs to neither. It does not compose part of the mother's body, but is a separate, self directing being. Although at conception and in the early stages of pregnancy this new collection of cells is very tiny, it already has a stored knowledge equivalent to 50 times the information contained in the *Encyclopedia Britannica*.[8] Certain cells are destined to become the body parts of the new person. The bulk of its development occurs in the first few weeks of pregnancy.

By two weeks of pregnancy the mother's period stops and the embryo is beginning to look less like a cluster of cells. By week three the heart beats and the foundations for the brain and nervous system are established. At four weeks the spinal cord and muscles are forming. Arms, legs, eyes and ears begin to show. At one month it is 10,000 times larger than the original fertilized cell. The heart pumps blood around the embryo's circulatory system and the placenta continues to provide nutrition and disposal of waste products. The mother's blood carries nutrients and oxygen through the placenta, passing into the developing embryo.

At 35 days of pregnancy fingers can be seen on the hands. Pigment is produced in the eyes. At 40 days brain waves can be detected and recorded. At 42 days the liver is functioning and producing blood cells. The brain begins to control the muscles and other organs. At 49 days the embryo can move its limbs. The jaw forms, including the buds which will form teeth in the gums. Eyelids seal to protect the developing, light-sensitive eyes. They re-open at about seven months gestation.

By the time the foetus is eight weeks old it is just over one inch long, and looks like a baby. All the organs are present and a normal baby at this stage will have a body as complete as that of a normal mature adult. The heart has been beating for over a month, and can be heard by ultra-sonic stethoscope. The kidneys begin to function and the stomach produces digestive juices. Muscles and nervous system are functioning and the foetus can respond to touch. At this stage it can suck its thumb and grasp at implements placed in the palm of its hands.[9] The foetus moves with a swimmer's stroke in the amniotic fluid that surrounds and protects it while it develops in the womb.

It is not quite known when the foetus starts to feel pain. Research has indicated that there may be some higher brain activity, including consciousness, as early as eight weeks gestation.[10] Other material suggests that although the foetus has a nervous system, pain cannot be felt until late in the pregnancy because there is no connection between the thalamus and the developing neocortex until then.[11] Doctors at Queen Charlotte's and Chelsea Hospital, London, carried out a study which concluded that unborn babies might feel pain and would require anaesthetic or painkillers prior to a blood test or transfusion. Dr Vivette Glover said that 'a foetus of 23 weeks gestation had a very clear pain response. At the moment people carry out abortions as if the foetus does not feel pain'. Glover *et al.* reported that they had measured hormonal stress responses in foetuses aged between 23 and 40 weeks old. Hormonal responses were compared during life-saving blood transfusions to the liver and transfusions to the umbilical cord, which has no nerves: 'The human foetus definitely mounts a significant hormonal stress response . . . it amounts to a stimuli that you or I or a child would find painful.' [12] Until relatively recently, it was believed that new born and premature babies did not feel pain. However, similar hormonal stress responses were found in such infants, and now medical practice demands that they are given analgesia before undergoing a medical procedure that may cause pain.

At nine weeks the foetus has finger prints. At ten weeks it can swallow and squint. At eleven weeks it is about two inches long, the muscles are more co-ordinated and urination occurs. At twelve weeks the foetus sleeps and awakens, as it will when born and for the rest of its life. It moves its muscles frequently, opens and closes its mouth, turns its head and can make a fist with its hand if the hand is stimulated. Amniotic fluid is breathed, the action of which develops the respiratory system. At thirteen weeks a fine down grows on its head and body. Its gender is obvious. At four months gestation, when eight to ten inches long, its movements may be felt by its mother. The ears are functioning and there is evidence that the foetus can hear some sounds, for example, the mother's heart beat, and external noises. It can respond to music.

At five months, when 12 inches long, its movements are clearly felt by its mother. It becomes startled by loud sounds or stress felt by the mother. It is argued that the foetus will respond to the feelings of the mother: if she is relaxed it will relax, if she is distressed it becomes startled and unrelaxed. [13] At six months the foetus is covered with a waxy substance, the vernix, which protects its skin from amniotic fluid. If born at this stage it can survive if given intensive care.

At seven months the foetus uses all its senses. It can recognize the sound of its mother's voice. [14] In the last few weeks of pregnancy the skin thickens, and fat is stored up for insulation and nourishment. Antibodies are increased. The foetus usually changes position ready for birth by turning so that the head is downwards at the cervix. At nine months the foetus is ready for birth.

The process of growth in a human being begins at conception and it is not complete until adulthood. Birth is just a milestone in the life of a person. [15] A born child is not complete in its development, for example, and there is an enormous change and development at adolescence. It could be argued that a neo-nate is not fully human, in much the same way as an embryo or foetus is often described. Simply because the neo-nate is not a fully grown, mature person we do not, on the whole, advocate killing him or her. [16] Likewise, a toddler or person in middle childhood is not fully developed. Because she is not fully developed does not mean that she has any less human rights than a mature human being.

CONCEALING KNOWLEDGE

Foetus and embryo are medical terms used to describe the unborn being. Terms such as uterine contents or the products of conception are often used when the foetus is destined for abortion. These terms make abortion more acceptable by obscuring the real truth about what abortion actually involves. It is, after all, far easier to accept the removal of a cluster of cells from the body than it is to accept that a very tiny human is being removed and killed in the process. Inhumane and cruel practices are far easier to carry out if the victim is dehumanized, or in the case of an animal, not valued as a living creature with feelings of pain, fear and distress. Devaluing starts with the language used. Soldiers will find it easier to kill those they call 'the enemy' and civilian deaths are more acceptable as 'collateral damage'. In the meat trade it is more lucrative for meat to be wrapped clinically in cellophane in the deep freezers of supermarkets, or concealed in a pie or a stew, than it is for them to be hung up as dead animals in the shop windows. Many meat eaters that I know remark that they do not think of meat as having once been alive. They do not think of its distress in the slaughter house because, when they purchase it, clean, clinical, wrapped up so nicely, it does not really resemble the corpse of a dead creature.

News reports and articles on the suffering of living animals in transit to other countries, or in battery farms, have caused many meat eaters to rethink their position on the rights of animals destined to be killed for food. The meat trade would not like the public to be educated about the truth of what happens in meat production, and in this they are very much like pro-abortion groups and some of the medical establishment, who would and do deny the public education on the nature of the foetus, foetal development, and what actually occurs during the seemingly easy, straight-forward and clinical procedure of an abortion. Pro-abortion material explaining the procedure does not tell the public (and especially a woman contemplating it) what happens to an unborn child during the operation. It cleverly skirts around that issue, describing it in much the same way as having a tooth or appendix removed.

If organizations claim to be 'pro-choice', then surely a woman has a right to a fully informed choice. She needs access to the whole truth, full details of what would happen to her baby, her own body and her psyche after abortion. Yet scientific fact is contradicted to keep people from knowledge that might lead to reconsideration of the issue. One example is an editorial that appeared in the feminist magazine *Everywoman* in May 1993, criticizing the pro-life movement (which of course it has a democratic right to do.) However, to be valid, criticism must be based on facts, not on propaganda, exaggerations or untruths.

The controversial film *The Silent Scream* was criticized. The writer claimed that a twelve-week-old foetus has no brain. This claim is quite simply, false. At twelve weeks' gestation, the brain of a normal foetus is fully intact and is functioning and producing brain waves. Everywoman claimed that the foetus is unable to scream because at twelve weeks it has 'no mouth, let alone lungs'. This is, again, untrue. These false claims made by a feminist magazine in effect dupe its readers, intelligent women from whom facts should not be suppressed. The editorial could have declared that it was debatable as to whether a foetus of this age can feel pain, or whether its lungs are developed enough to scream. Judging from this editorial, either the writer was ignorant of foetal development and had made no effort to find out, or the magazine was blatantly printing untruths to deceive women. Yet, it is only when the truth of an issue is out that people can begin to question, to search for ways to avoid violence, killing, oppression and cruelty.

FOETAL RIGHTS

Having established that a foetus is clearly human, and not just 'potentially' human or an inanimate cluster of cells, the issue is whether it has the same rights as a fully developed human. Is a small, developing embryo equal to an adult woman? Does it acquire human rights at a certain stage of gestation? Jenny Morris believes that once a foetus, disabled or non-disabled, is viable outside its mother's body, its right to life are greater than its mother's rights to refuse to give birth to it.[17] She also believes that feminists have been forced into denying that the unborn child has any human status. She cites Wendy Savage, pro-abortion gynaecologist and obstetrician, who agrees with anti-abortionists that life begins at conception and a new individual starts, believing that performing abortion differs from other surgery because the foetus is, to her, a potential human being.[18] Savage poses the issue in terms of balancing conflicting rights between mother and child: 'As the foetus becomes larger, its rights become greater, and there comes a point . . . where the foetus's right to live equals the right to get the pregnancy terminated.' Some feminists clearly believe there is a difference between aborting a foetus of early, and one of late gestation, even if others fought vehemently against the Alton Bill in 1987, winning partial success as abortion of disabled foetuses up to birth is now permitted.

With regard to Savage's belief that there comes a point when a foetus's right to live equals the mother's right to abort, the question must be asked, when is that point? At what stage does a foetus 'become' human, and at what stage is a foetus to be considered 'unhuman' enough to abort it?

Can it be more justifiable to kill something or someone because it is smaller or less developed? I may kill a fly, even though I am a vegetarian, because I may believe the germs it carries presents a threat to me, though I would not kill a fly for the sake of it. Some women may feel this way about an unplanned pregnancy, threatened and frightened (especially where a woman has been raped or coerced into sex). I might believe that an abortifacient taken before implantation has occurred is acceptable, but once a embryo has developed, he or she has an equal right to protection from death as that of an older foetus. If one argues that a larger baby has more right to life than a smaller baby, does this also apply to a child outside the womb? A person arguing for protection for an older or larger foetus may use the viability argument to justify this view. However, no young child can survive outside the womb unless it is totally cared for by an adult. And it is equally as wrong to kill a dependent child as it is to kill an independent, fully developed adult. Being a foetus, something every single one of us has been, is merely another stage of human development, like babyhood, childhood, adolescence, adulthood, and old age. The age and size of a foetus is therefore irrelevant when considering whether or not it has human rights.

SENTIENCE

It is often argued that it is wrong to kill a sentient, thinking being, so that if a living thing is not capable of thinking or perception of senses there is nothing wrong with ending such a life. Those who defend meat eating and vivisection see animals as a lower form of life, unable to think or reason like humans, and those who defend abortion and euthanasia see foetuses and infants in the same way.

But animals feel pain. Pull a dog's tail and it will yelp in distress. Some species of animal are more developed than others, but should a higher place on the evolutionary scale confer more rights on an animal?[19] Development of a human personality is gradual but sure, as it experiences learning and stimulation throughout its life. If intelligence and sentience at any one moment is criteria to allow life, then how sentient, how intelligent must an individual be, and who defines those criteria? And where do the notions of allowing life on the basis of sentience and intelligence leave disabled people? Eugenic arguments that learning disabled people can lawfully be killed before or after birth was the thinking behind the euthanasia programme of the Third Reich. It is argued, even today, that killing a person who will never fulfill arbitrarily defined criteria of intelligence is a benevolent act: that people with profound disabilities, reliant on others for care and assistance, are better off dead, whether by abortion or euthanasia. To genuine concern over pain, limitations and distress is often added the belief that such people are incapable of feelings or rational thought.

But this is very judgmental of another person's life. People are all different in development and abilities, and notions of intelligence and personality vary. Why should only the intelligent live? Are we all to sit IQ tests before we are granted this basic right? Then where will it stop? If we use sentience and intelligence as criteria for the granting of life, then why not use physical appearance, colour, race, class and age?

CONCLUSION

If something is capable of suffering then I would argue that it is wrong to cause it distress. We know enough about the foetus to be morally compelled to seriously consider at least, the pain and distress that may be caused in abortion at nearly all stages. For feminists in particular, this is a moral issue that must be explored as a matter of urgency.

I do not believe that making abortion 'illegal' is the answer to women's problems. Yet I am wholly against abortion. Working to prevent abortion is necessary, by reducing social demand through social reform, better sex education, availability of free, safe contraception, better child care facilities, not leaving responsibility and care of children to women alone. Women need help and support, before birth, during the child's life, maybe throughout a woman's whole life, though Western society, for example, frequently fails in this. Many women feel they have no choice but to abort. What feminists must do is to ensure that women do not have to resort to abortion. Many might dismiss this as idealism, but this could be said about peace or environmental campaigns or the women's movement itself. Just because a goal is difficult, does not mean we should not work towards it. After all, if it was futile to try and make things better, there would be no feminism.

NOTES

1 Numbers: 5:11–31.
2 *Lion Encyclopaedia of the Bible*, second edition (Lion Publishing, Oxford, 1989).
3 Exodus: 21:22–5.
4 Brennan, W., 'Female Objects of Semantic Dehumanization and Violence', *Studies in Pro-life Feminism*, vol. 1, no. 3 Summer 1995, 203–34.
5 David Alton's Private Member's Bill 1987.
6 *Pocket Dictionary for Nurses* (Oxford Medical Publications, Oxford).
7 Sometimes more than one ovum is released and each is fertilized by a sperm, giving rise to non-identical twins, or multiplicity of foetuses.
8 From, 'Human Life Begins at Conception . . . Human Rights Do Too'. *Newlife* leaflet available from Kay House, 51 Stonebridge Drive, Frome, BA11 2TW.
9 Nilson, L., *The Everyday Miracle: A Child Is Born* (Allen Lane,London, 1967).
10 Odelbad, E., 'Consciousness in the Child in Utero: a Short Presentation of Recent Research', presented at 'The Splintered Image' *Conference at the Pollock Halls*, Edinburgh, 27–30 August, 1987.
11 See Dworkin, R., *Life's Dominion: An Argument about Abortion and Euthanasia* (Harper Collins, London, 1995), 17–18.
12 Fisk, N. Glover, V., 'Confronting the Issue of Foetal Pain: Pain Relief for the Foetus Not Just for the Preterm Baby?', letter to *British Medical Journal*, March 1996.
13 Newlife information Sheet, 'Human Life Begins at Conception . . .', op cit.
14 Nilson L., op cit.
15 The lack of significance of birth on the nervous system is particularly relevant. Dr R.M. Case, in his text book *Variations in Human Physiology* (Manchester University Press, 1985, 6) tells us: 'Birth is of little significance in the development of the nervous system. Although it is possible to plot growth velocity curves and to present a timetable of myelination, the process is a continuous one' from conception to full maturity; birth is merely an incidental milestone along the way. . . .'
16 There are, however, those philosophers who do advocate the killing of newborns such as Peter Singer (see conclusion), believing that we should have, in law, an arbitrarily set period in which

infants are not designated persons until officially invested with the title, allowing infanticide, specifically of handicapped children.

17 Morris, J., *Pride against Prejudice: Transforming Attitudes to Disability* (The Women's Press, London, 1991), 74.

18 Savage quoted in Himmelweit, S., 'More Than a Woman's Right To Choose?', *Feminist Review*, No. 29, Spring 1988, 50.

19 The argument that we should include apes in our moral 'community of equals' is expounded by Peter Singer and others in the book *The Great Ape Project: Equality beyond Humanity* (Fourth Estate, London, 1993). But in Singer's reasoning, a healthy ape has more 'right' to life than a handicapped baby.

6

Abortion and Disability: Is That Different?

MARIE-CLAIRE DARKE

'That's different?' is what most women and feminists would say when questioned about the elimination of one particular social group, the disabled, through abortion and infanticide. The abortion of female offspring in many Asian countries because they are seen as undesirable, is, it is argued, a different matter as well. The mass infanticide of female babies in China, because they are expensive to marry off, that's different also. But is it that different? Of course not, it is just a convenient phrase to ignore the genocide of a group of people that we don't want in our society.

The reasoning many people in other cultures give for killing female offspring is the same as those used here to not have a disabled child: cost, stigma, burden, their marriage potential, etc. etc.

The excuses are the same; excuses that are all equally invalid for the elimination of a female child as they are for the elimination of a disabled child. Such similarities in reasoning can be explained and understood if we assume that Aristotle's notion of there being a hierarchy of physical perfection, with the male human form being at the summit, is the basis of most western beliefs on the value and position of women. Consequently, therefore, the female represents the first step along the road to deformity;[1] making the elimination of women as eugenically pleasing as the disposal of disabled people in a patriarchal society (ours, in other words).

Let me make various points clear before I elaborate any further on this. The abortion and infanticide of disabled foetuses is seen legally, and therefore medically, socially and politically, as something quite distinct to that of the 'ordinary' foetus and baby. No other foetus or baby has the struggle to survive that the disabled baby does. This is not because of its disability but because of the social, state and medical structures put in place to weed it out, 'weed' being an appropriate metaphor for how the disabled individual is seen and the attitude of the medical profession in its treatment of a disabled person: kill it. Under the 1990 Human Fertilisation and Embryology Act, primarily, there is no time limit in which an abortion must be carried out. Suspected disability is reason enough for carrying out an abortion. Combined with this, infanticide, through non-treatment of disabled babies, is routine and based solely on subjectively dubious notions of 'quality of life'. Such actions, attitudes and policies would be totally unacceptable if applied to any other social group. If the child was treated in such a way solely on the grounds that they were, for example, black, or Asian, or female, or red-haired or brown-eyed, or Jewish, or Catholic, serious questions about our perceptions of our society and ourselves would be asked. But not if the child has Spina Bifida, not if it has Down's Syndrome or Cerebral Palsy![2]

Mary Douglas argued that disabled people make us uneasy as they threaten our sense of mastery over nature;[3] a fact which partly explains the medical profession's obsession with eradicating the disabled as a group, though not the average woman's equal desire and participation in that eradication. That is much more complex; the pressure we, as women, are put under to collude in the medico-cleansing of society is both explicit and easily inferred in a variety of complex social relations.

When I had my son I had expected to be put under considerable pressure to test (and abort) for foetal abnormality; my husband has severe Spina Bifida and Hydrocephalus; he is obviously congenitally deformed to anyone who meets him. I was not prepared for the assumptions and pressures that I would be put under, and not only from the medical profession but our families and friends also. My refusal to have any tests often resulted in a brow-beating from medical staff, indignation from relatives and abuse and bafflement from others. I wanted to say to our 'friends', so many times, 'I thought you liked Paul?' It seemed, and is, so illogical that someone could be a friend and yet presume we would find it abhorrent to bring another being into existence who might be like my husband; on the contrary, it was, for me, quite a nice idea; after all, I love my husband for who and what he is, not despite him being what he is. To divorce the body from the character is not only reductive but a fallacy that is farcical.

I was not aware of the degree to which people are able to divorce a contradictory reality from their own generalized fantasies, that is, the 'disabled' as a generalized Other, whilst seeing my husband as something quite distinct from them, the disabled, in general. It is hard to convince people that their opinions about the generalised Other, the disabled in general, have a very real affect on the everyday lives, not least the confidence, of individual disabled people.

The indirect social pressure that is put upon women to have tests for foetal abnormality – which carry with them an implicit acceptance that the 'wrong' result will result in an abortion –is all around us. The cut backs in social services tell us that if we have an impaired child the responsibility will rest with us as parents. Media images tell us that the disabled life is a sad one and that the disabled are 'rightly' segregated.[4] The news tells us how tragic it is to be disabled in its nightly stories of the search for a cure for disabilities (that has never happened). Our parents tell us nightmare tales of families who did have a 'crippled child' in the past. The nightmare is portrayed all around us and we accept its truth unthinkingly, and unaware-aware of its false content or the social reasons for its elements of truth. Our very ignorance of the reality of disability and its social construction encourage us to participate in the destruction of a social group as vital, real and valid, as ourselves. The actual existence of a test to discover an abnormality implies, very strongly, that such impairments or eventualities are to be avoided at all cost; if the state has seen fit to invest so much money, time and effort to not only creating the test but offering mass screening, then the actual impairment must be pretty bloody awful, irrespective of what the professional says to the expectant mother. Such hidden state coercion is immense and very real but, none the less, socially constructed. As Troy Duster has written:

> Genetic counsellors are probably, as professionals, indeed neutral, if this means that they do as much as possible not to communicate their personal prejudices and opinions about whether a couple should take a chance or not or whether they would recommend living with a disability or not, etc. However, the individual neutrality of the counsellor is not the issue. It is, in fact, the machinery of a screen that has been erected. Even if one is neutral about whether or not one uses the advice or technology, etc., the simple fact that the screen is in place communicates a powerful message that something is wrong with the disorder for which the screen is in place.

Duster then continues, even more ominously, that:

> Once a test is available and a woman decides not to use it, if her baby is born with a disability that could have been diagnosed. It is no longer an act of fate but has become her own fault.[5]

Consequently, I would argue, the passive acceptance of the routine abortion of impaired or abnormal foetuses not only inhibits real freedom of choice but ensures that choice is systematically withdrawn from women making a decision about having a baby with an impairment. By extension, it also continues, supports and further perpetrates the processes of disablement that any impaired individual, and their mother, will face in the near and distant future.

The call of nature, the call to nature is often made to justify our genocidal attitudes to disability — what else can the 80% abortion rate of people with Spina Bifida be called — just as it was in the subjugation of women for thousands of years. And, as with women, just because we were told it for thousands of years did not make it any less wrong; and, as with women, just because many of us lived our lives as parodies of the male ideal of women, it still did not make it right. We, women, fought a battle for equality on the grounds that biology is not destiny and now we apply that determinist tag to another group who only seek equality: nothing more and nothing less. Just as we were accused of wanting special treatment and favours, we now accuse the disabled of wanting special favours and treatment.

One of the main criticisms of disabled people against the routine acceptance of the abortion of an impaired foetus is, as I stated above, that the basis on which it is carried out — the presumed low 'quality of life' thesis — is wrong. There are two points to be made here; firstly, that often the information given to a potential parent of an impaired child is drawn from a nightmare scenario that will rarely actually come in to being. A strong enough point in itself but one which can be used against disabled people; what if the infant may actually fulfil the definition of a low 'quality of life' by most people's standards: does this then make it an OK thing to do? I would argue here that it would still not be a reasonable thing to do because it is still based upon a subjective view (even if it is 'most' people's view). The point is that if we wish to value difference we must value all difference and not just that which might closely resemble our own standards of life and living.

The key reason for rejecting any 'quality of life' arguments is that it is rooted in a medicalized pathological view of what it is to be alive; impaired or not. It ignores the social factors of existence, factors which are intrinsically more important that the pathology of the individual because we may live life within an individual body but we experience society and culture through its social constructions which are liable and capable of dramatic change. In a society where steps, ignorance and fear abound being in a wheelchair is hard; all those things are constructs through which we live our lives. They can change or be eradicated; therefore such a society could exist that meant being in a wheelchair was non-problematic.

To constantly place the burden of impairment on the individual is not only a social lie, but a misrepresentation of how we all live our lives: it is mediated, constructed and ultimately defined by the social structures (constructions) which define our thoughts, feelings and actions. We must move away from seeing everything as the problem of the individual (the medical model of disability) and start to see it as it really is, a social construct we have created for one reason or another. If you have ever pushed a wheelchair you soon realise the problems that a wheelchair user faces; not because they are in a wheelchair but because of actual physical man-made construction which inhibits a wheelchair user's full partici- pation in society and its many cultural manifestations.

The medical model of women has been used against us for centuries (biology as destiny) but we have resisted it to show that being a woman does not mean a single thing but a rich variety of experiences that are as influenced as much by culture as anything else. No feminist would argue, I hope, that it is the same to be a black woman as it is to a white one, or that to be a working-class woman is the same as being a middle-class one. There are some shared experienced (denigration by society for a physical reality: sex), as there are for disabled people (denigration by 'normal' people) but just like women, their experiences, perspec- tives and lives are as rich, varied and as sad as ours. Yes, sad. Many people lead sad lives; it is not due to a pathological state but a social constraint or imprison- ment usually. But it is as equally valid to be sad and pathetic as it is to be admired and successful as, more often than not, it has nothing to do with your body but the circumstances in which you live.

There is a 'quality of life' test my husband always finds somewhat amusing because if applied to him and then the rest of society, most of the rest of society has to be put down immediately. Social circumstances have dictated this, not any intrinsic ability: he has a car, a house, a PhD, a son, regular holidays, is respected by his friends and community – even if they would kill any one who might be born like him – he has money to do what ever he pleases, he is on national and regional committees and selection panels and, most importantly, he has me. Most things which the majority of the population would spend their lives trying to achieve and still fail to get. Why? Good fortune, affluent relatives, luck and an ability to appease white middle class culture by parodying it. Yet, if born today, he would have been aborted or left to die by a doctor who would have told his parents that they had entered the nightmare scenario.

It is a mistake to assume that I am arguing that disabled people should not be routinely killed because my husband ended up not being a nightmare scenario; circumstances and individuals in his life might have been different – I might have listened to all those people who were telling me I was making the worst mistake of my life (that was listening to them in the first place). That is my point really: the line between being one of 'them' or one of 'us' is a fine one, not only for them, but for us also. Accidents of birth define our lives: being born disabled in a middle-class family is often more beneficial than being born able-bodied and working-class or poor. Money is often a bigger determinant of disability that your actual impairment ever is.

This all begs the question of what purpose does the extermination of one particular group serve. I would argue that it is two fold; one is a financial and the other more social (but not psychological). The cost-benefit analysis work that has been undertaken and used by most Western governments has proved that disabled people can cost society more than the ordinary 'Jo/e'. This can be looked at in two ways: one, it may be the case occasionally, but is rarely so, and would even be less so if society was constructed more equally to enable disabled people to participate on an equal footing. But, secondly, it would be a mistake to argue this point too much because some people with impairments will always cost more (rightly so) for the state to manage and provide for. So what? If you base your view of life on cash cost you will get the society you deserve; as activists we should make those who define life like this make it explicit rather than let them hide behind the falsehoods of dubious claims to nature and 'quality of life' scales.

Another point to be made about the excessive cost of disability, which is often a very real extra cost, should not be ignored, because it otherwise leads the 'ordinary Jo/e' (i.e. the non-disabled person) to think that s/he costs the state and society nothing. We all cost money and massive government expenditure is spent on able-bodied white middle class people such as myself everyday for the preservation of our 'quality of life' at the expense of others. The massive subsidisation of private health care (through state funded research, tax conces- sions, the use of NHS equipment, premises and training) is a prime example. Private health care is not available to sick and disabled people as it is too expensive yet we, as a small minority of its funders, reap all the benefits. Private education is largely state-funded yet those who benefit from it pay very little for it. The laws of natural selection are as often applied to the few who benefit as the many who are slain by it; but as E.P. Thompson argued, the claim to natural laws are the greatest evasion of truth used by the middle-classes to hide, ignore and exploit social inequality for their own purposes.[6] That is why the eugenics movement has, and always will be, class and male dominated. The apparent 'common sense' of such claims to natural laws are so attractive because they seem to absolve those who participate in their conclusions from any blame, but as we all know, 'common sense' is as equally socially constructed as the M25; like the M25, it did not just come in to existence, it was built over a very long period of time, until it seemed like it had always been there (cf. the work of Gramsci).

Feminists have often argued that it is the women's right to choose and, it could be said, as a feminist who am I to argue against that? That is not at stake here as often those who are making a decision about whether or not to abort an apparently impaired foetus desperately want a child, or are in the process of building what they see as their family; and by the way, many a wanted 'normal' infant is exterminated in the obsessive zeal to eradicate the abnormal ones. We must not forget that the issue of whether or not to abort a disabled child is much more complex than merely 'the right to choose'. Most abortions of impaired foetuses are only ever an issue for women who want a baby because they are not usually discovered until later in a pregnancy, at a time when those who choose an abortion have long had one.

It would also be wrong to assume that I am being critical of women who have abortions of impaired children, I am not directly. Considering the pressure that these women face, politically, socially and through the media, along with the desperately tragic (false) image that is given of life with an impairment, it is quite understandable. It is wrong of any individual, disabled or not, to criticise any individual woman who has an abortion on the basis of suspected or real impairment to the foetus; to do so would be to indulge in the individualizing of what is a social pressure reinforced by its culture and politics. To individualize the problem disabled people face in society's determination to be rid of them is to do to others that which society is doing to them: individualize and de-politicize a social and political issue.

Abortion is, like disability, a social construct; a set of ideological beliefs and structures that are not simply 'there' but a complex system of socio-cultural and political options utilized among and above other equally ideological options. One of the aims of this book is to flesh out the seemingly 'natural' claims that many of the old feminist rallying calls called upon; putting them in to a wider context and enabling us all to make more informed judgements upon the basis of a wider realisation of the nuances of the female experience and not just based upon the white-middle class calls to a narrow band of liberal bourgeois education or information.

So what is the ultimate function, I am if nothing else a terrible functionalist, of aborting a disability? I would argue that it defines normality for a consumer culture dependent upon perpetuating the myth that it actually exists. As Georges Canguilhem wrote: 'strictly speaking a norm does not exist; it plays its role which is to devalue existence by allowing its correction' .[7] He continues, much further on, with his usual astute grasping of the realities of the relationship between the normal and the abnormal, stating that: 'it is not paradoxical to say that the abnormal, while logically second, is existentially first'.[8] What Canguilhem is saying, later elaborated on by Michel Foucault, is that rather than abnormality actually being a deviation from a norm, it actually defines the norm where none existed before.

Bailey (1996) almost makes this point, without fully realising the complexity – or is it the simplicity – of the process, when she writes that it 'does seem that the institutional practice of prenatal testing systematically separates the normal from the "abnormal", and brings in to play a whole set of different judgements about the future for the latter as compared with the former'.[9] Those different set of judgements can only actually exist if you separate two groups of people from day one; the abnormal is first, it defines the limits and parameters of normality for that moment and the future.

As we live in a consumerist culture where the only true value of humanity is based upon the number of commodities we have; the more 'normal' we are the more commodities, we are told, we can obtain. In fact, we have to buy many commodities just to maintain our illusions of normality, even if that is at the expense of the natural: e.g. deodorant. This is especially true for women: the pressure to control our bodies and weight is the best example of this process. Failure to control and maintain our normality is seen as not only a social wrong but a sign of moral turpitude. And as that is for the male gaze, the extermination of the abnormal is for their dubious moral gaze. Yet again we are complicit in the denigration of difference for a patriarchal structure.

Under the Nazi's a quarter of a million disabled people were exterminated under their racial hygiene laws;[10] modern western countries in total carry out an equal number of exterminations per year for the same reasons: economics, supposed burden to the state, spurious 'quality of life' arguments and a false notion of normality as superior to abnormality. Modern technological advances used in the detection of abnormality are the full flowering of a fascist ideology against our own bodies. Should we be complicit in that body fascist hegemony?

Abortion of any kind is never a simplistic issue or decision and the issue of the abortion of impaired foetuses is even more complex but, sadly, it is often too simple a decision. Disability, the resulting social exclusion of an individual based upon their physical limitation (one's impairment), is not as simple an issue as it is portrayed; it is a social and political issue, much like abortion, and it is not about individuals or their experience of their impairment, the argument that Morris[11] and others would make.

For an excellent elaboration of the difference between impairment and disability see Michael Oliver's two books.[12] That is not to say that the experience of impairment does not have its place, but it is a different issue to disability politics and something which enables those who wish to denigrate disabled people much greater chance to do so as it reintroduces the scope for an individualising attitude towards disabled people as a marginalised socio-political group (male and female). It is an intellectual weakness that presumes that the feminist dimension cannot be incorporated in to the overall disability politics argument without resorting to 'impairment' orientated examples or philosophies which re-individualises impairment as disability. Just as it is atavistic to blame individual women who have abortions of impaired foetuses it is reactionary, and ultimately self defeating, to argue for the reintroduction of impairment in to disability politics.

In conclusion, I would argue that many feminists accept the social propaganda used against disabled people without question, and I hope that this short chapter goes some way in making other feminists think about it a little more seriously. Feminism is, by its very nature, about the validation of difference and Otherness – the female as 'the first step on the road along abnormality'. All I am doing is arguing that we go down that road a little further and pick up a few more allies and friends; if for no other reason than the fact that half of the disabled community are our sisters.

NOTES

1 Garland, R., 'Deformity and Disfigurement in the Graeco-Roman World', *History Today*, November 1992, 39–44.
2 See Bailey, R., 'Prenatal Testing and the Prevention of Impairment: A Woman's Right to Choose?', Morris, J. (ed.), *Encounters with Strangers: Feminism and Disability* (The Woman's Press, London,1996), 143–67, for a fuller examination of these points.
3 Douglas, M., *Purity and Danger* (Routledge, London, 1966).
4. Darke, P., 'The Cinematic Construction of Disability', unpublished PhD thesis at the University of Warwick, Coventry, 1996.
5 Duster, T., *Backdoor to Eugenics* (Routledge, London, 1990), 227.
6 Mazumdar, P.M., *Eugenics, Human Genetics and Human Failings: The Eugenics Society, Its Sources and Its Critics in Britain* (Routledge, London,1992).
7 Canguilhem, G., *The Normal and the Pathological* (Zone Books, New York,1989), 77.
8 Canguilhem, ibid, 243.
9 Bailey, op.cit., 152.
10 Gallagher, H., *By Trust Betrayed: Patients, Physicians and the License to Kill in the Third Reich* (Henry Holt, New York,) 1990.
11 Morris, J. (ed.), *Encounters with Strangers: Feminism and Disability* (Women's Press, London, 1996).
12 Oliver, M., *The Politics of Disablement* (Macmillan, London, 1990), and Oliver, M., *Understanding Disability* (Macmillan, London, 1996).

7

Is Abortion Good for Women?

RACHEL MAC NAIR

THE DECISION

Sandra Bensing was desperate to get her children out of foster care. Her husband was in prison, she was poor, and pregnant. She went to her local public defenders to get help in getting her children back. Noting her advanced pregnancy, attorney Margie Pitts Hames believed that this would make an excellent test case. So she got her into a case known as *Doe v. Bolton*. Whereas the *Roe v. Wade* case in 1973 struck down practically all laws regulating or prohibiting abortion in the United States, *Doe* specifically approved abortion in the third trimester. But Sandra Bensing had never even wanted an abortion, was utterly appalled at the idea).[1]

Norma McCorvey, however, did want an abortion. As Jane Roe, Norma was pleased with the outcome of *Roe v. Wade*. She needed the abortion, she said, because she had no job, no child care, no prospects. Her attorneys used her as a test case without attempting to secure her any of those.[2]

The 'right to choose' is meaningless with only one choice. Women do not 'find' themselves pregnant, catch pregnancy like colds. For every child conceived by a consenting woman, there is somewhere a man with an equal part in making that baby, every bit as responsible for its well-being as the woman. When abortion is sanctioned, many men see a baby resulting not from their actions, but from the woman's decision not to abort. If the baby's existence is all her decision, then they see it as her responsibility. They believe they are not liable for child support payments. So they don't make them.

Those payments are only the legal requirement. Morally, they should be equally responsible for nappy changing as well, and all the other work that goes into raising children. Conversely, there are very good, loving, nurturing fathers who would be delighted to take their equal parenting role. But abortion serves a double punch against feminist attempts to encourage men to be gentle, tender responsible fathers, while discouraging those men who are told to put their emotions about their children on hold until the woman makes a decision.

Presuming that pregnant women should make decisions alone places them in social isolation, robbing them of support they need and have a right to. The workplace, for example, may refuse to accommodate her on the grounds that the pregnancy is 'her project'. When an unexpected pregnancy is treated as a medical problem, rather than an ordinary female circumstance, a woman's choice becomes more and more constricted by the prejudices of people who wonder why she is inconveniencing them when she could have had an abortion.

Even medical ignorance has been used to insist on women's need for abortion. There are common antibiotics, for example, that severely decrease the effectiveness of oral contraceptives. If a woman does not know this and subsequently becomes pregnant, it can be argued that she has lost control. But she can maintains control only when her basic right to information about such side effects is respected by her doctors. Her control is not regained by abortion.

Frederica Mathewes-Green has said that a woman does not want an abortion like she wants an ice cream cone, or a Porsche. She wants an abortion like an animal, caught in a trap, wants to gnaw its leg off in order to get free of the trap.[3] The remark was actually used by pro-abortion columnists and activists, unaware that the remark came from a pro-life source. To them, it showed how utterly necessary abortion is. But if an animal is caught in a trap, it does not need an offer of surgical amputation. The kind and just thing to do is to let the animal out of that trap. Even better yet, ensure there is no trap. So many women see abortion as an act of desperation, and the so-called pro-choice position only tells them to experience their despair in a sterile surrounding instead of a filthy one. Abortion, resulting from injustice, perpetuates injustice. It tells women not to be so uppity as to counter the injustice, but instead to accommodate it.

THE PRACTICE

A student nurse in an obstetric hospital was asked by the doctor she worked with what her birth control arrangements were. She told him she didn't need any. Later that day, he asked her to come with him, and not to ask him where they were going. Her affidavit states, and medical reports confirmed, that he raped her there.[4] He performed large numbers of abortions. Yet her sovereignty over her body on this occasion was not his motivation. A 'woman's right to choose' to have an abortion made it unnecessary for him to respect her right to choose not to have sex with him.

The argument is frequently made that, whether one opposes abortion or not, it will occur, therefore should occur under sanitary, medical conditions, rather than at the hands of 'back street butchers'. For people of compassion, this is the most effective argument there is for abortion legalization. Leaving aside the question of whether more abortions actually occur when it is legal, the question still remains as to whether legalization has ensured women's safety. Does legal abortion practice attract proportionately more scrupulous practitioners ? Does legalization prevent sexual misconduct, alcohol or drug problems, or negligence?

Abu Hayat, a doctor in New York City, severed a child's arm in an unsuccessful abortion attempt. Several other botches finally led to his license being revoked. Citing one case of abuse means little, of course: every specialty has its bad apples.

But disturbingly, Barbara Radford, the executive director of the National Abortion Federation, commented that: 'Physicians like Hayat can be found in every city in the United States'.[5] These were not the words of raving right-to-life fanatics, but the spokesperson of the association of abortion clinics, quoted in a magazine which defends abortion regularly.

Images of women endangering their own lives in frantic pursuit of abortions is used to insist on making abortions available. The book *The Worst of Times* quotes a law enforcement officer:

> There was one thing I never understood. These women were having abortions done with coat hangers, under horrible conditions, and the women I would see in hospitals were in terrible shape. Hell, enough of them were sick enough to die! But they wouldn't talk. They simply wouldn't tell who did it or where it was done. I'd plead with a woman to tell me, and she would just look away or turn her head to the wall. Even when they thought that they might die, they wouldn't tell. That just made no sense to me. If one of those people who did the abortion had robbed her on the street or done any other criminal act, she would have told, real quick. But there sure was something different about this. No one talked about it, especially the women. In those days, a lot of women were losing their lives or their health as a result of abortions, but still they wouldn't talk. Why?[6]

This must have occurred to many people. A possible answer to this question is that, at that time, cases of rape and what was called 'wife-beating' were also poorly prosecuted. Women were not inclined to take those cases to court either. The defence in all those cases often attacked the victim savagely, and it was often difficult to get the prosecutors interested.

If rapists and wife-beaters are ignored, then the pattern is certainly set for abortion abuses as well. In all three cases, a vigorous prosecution might follow if the woman actually died. Failing that, the amount of abuse of women that was tolerated was appalling.

How often does a woman actually blame herself for getting pregnant? She must deal with an arrogant, overwhelmingly male medical establishment. Often, she is embarrassed, as if she had made a mistake or gotten caught at something. So she seeks out a way to sweep it all under the rug. She will accept lesser standards of care for doing so, as if she deserves no better. She is following the traditional sexist script of internal blame, letting others involved off the hook. This helps explain why mere legalization did not get rid of the horror stories. Women who would not tolerate mistreatment by any other doctor have endured shocking behaviour from abortionists.

This problem could be alleviated somewhat by greater monitoring of abortion doctors. Any moves in that direction are crucial for women's well-being. But the basic point remains; abortions are done by abortionists, and that alone should send a chill down the back of any woman undergoing the procedure. Some abortion doctors are better than others – that's true whether it's legal or not- but the horror stories of yesteryear have not stopped. Even when abortion is practised at its best, relatively free from the profit motive which might encourage women to abort, there remains a common feature that should startle any self-respecting feminist. Consciousness raising has always been important to the feminist cause: it is therefore extraordinary when deliberate ignorance is fostered in any institution that claims to be working for women's rights.

Nurse Sallie Tisdale worked in an abortion clinic and wrote of her experiences for *Harper's Magazine*:

> I am speaking in a matter of fact voice about 'the tissue' and 'the contents' when the woman suddenly catches my eye and asks, 'How big is the baby now?' These words suggest a quiet need for a definition of the boundaries being drawn. It isn't so odd, after all, that she feels relief when I describe the growing bud's bulbous shape, its miniature nature. Again I gauge, and sometimes lie a little, weaseling around its infantile features until its clinging power slackens. But when I look in the basin among the curdlike blood clots, I see an elfin thorax, attenuated, its penecilling ribs all in parallell rows with tiny knobs of spine rounding upwards. A translucent arm and hand swim beside.[7]

An article in the journal of the American Medical Association (the biggest organization of doctors), noted:

> Patients also sometimes ask to view the fetal remains. A Toronto physician said she didn't know 'how and whether we [should] protect the patient from the reality of the procedure. She said she regularly hid the ultrasound screen and 'whisked away' the 'fetal products'. 'She's probably not prepared for what she is going to see,' she said of the patient.[8]

The theme of deliberate ignorance is depressingly common in the literature:

> Besides its use in ascertaining fetal age, sonography can be very helpful during actual abortion procedures, both as a teaching tool and as a means of enhancing safety. But sonography in connection with induced abortion may have psychological hazards. Seeing a blown-up, moving image of the embryo she is carrying can be distressing to a woman who is about to undergo an abortion, Dr Dorfman noted. 'She stressed that the screen should be turned away from the patient'.[9]

Raising consciousness is a technique that, among other things, helps women locate and thereby eradicate undesirable behaviour, both in themselves and in those with whom they relate. When it is painstakingly avoided, women are treated as children rather than as trustworthy decision-making adults.

In theory, abortion *can* be practised by well-monitored doctors without excessive profit motive, with adequate information being given to potential clients. This happens in many countries, where consequently the abortion rate

decreases dramatically. Paying attention to the medical rights of women considering abortion decreases the number of abortions, just as paying attention to their
social, economic and political rights will. Women need information, not just
about foetal development and alternative services, but also the normal complications of abortion. So much emphasis has been put on making abortion 'safe
and legal' that many women forget that it is still surgery. Infection and haemor-
rhaging are common, occasional perforations lead to hysterectomies and similar
surgeries, an incompetent cervix or scarring of the uterine tissue, leading to
miscarriages of later wanted pregnancies, ectopic pregnancies, and premature
births.

These possible complications are not in dispute, although the frequency of
them is, since good long-term follow-up care is not commonplace. If a woman
dies from a hysterectomy or ectopic pregnancy, her death is attributed to those
causes and not to the abortion that caused those problems. Therefore, the actual
death rate from abortion remains unknown.

One possible complication remains a source of controversy: whether or not
abortion of a first pregnancy significantly increases the likelihood of breast
cancer. The hypothesis is that in a summarily terminated first pregnancy,
protective hormonal reactions within the breast may be adversely affected.
Abundant epidemiological evidence and individual studies of women matched
with control groups show this as a definite possibility. Abortion defenders
vociferously deny the link, arguing that other studies dispute this. The debate
continues and cannot be settled here. But women *need* it settled. There is
certainly enough evidence to warrant a definitive study: there is no wild goose
chase involved, no eccentric idea.

Tragically, groups interested in researching breast cancer seem to find their
support for abortion more important than their opposition to breast cancer at
this time. The question must be asked: why does support for abortion keep
interfering with women's rights?

THE AFTERMATH

Women who have aborted are a major constituency group of the pro-life
movement. This is remarkable, given that they must admit to having a child dead,
and having participated in making the child dead. Many would find these
admissions too painful, therefore avoiding the subject completely, or be especially belligerent on behalf of abortion availability. It is not odd that there are
women that insist that there is no pain, because that would be the case whether
or not there is. But many women do regard their own abortions as traumatic, and
this is not limited to women who have joined the pro-life movement. During a
phone-in radio interview a woman who underwent an abortion several years
earlier insisted that she had made the right decision. Yet the pain in her voice

was so obvious that I made reference to it without the remotest fear that there was anyone in the audience that had not caught it. It was not just her tone of voice; she referred to the incident as 'two hours of pain and humiliation'.

These expressions are not uncommon. Even abortion defenders will occasionally refer to the inherent undesirability of the matter, insisting that while it may be a tragedy, it is a necessity. A tragedy, of course, is not a right. If it is widespread for women to go through something painful and humiliating, is that not a scathing indictment of the anti-women nature of society? Even worse are those who insist abortion should not have emotional aftermath, and therefore does not. When confronted by a woman who is suffering, they respond that it was her choice and she should just learn to live with it. The term 'choice', which would otherwise sound so benevolent, becomes a cruel way of avoiding unpleasantness when faced with the real-world consequences of advocacy.

Joan Appleton worked as a counsellor in an abortion clinic for some time, and developed a lengthy questioning process:

> I counselled these women so well. They were so sure of their decision. Why are they coming back after me now, months and years later, psychological wrecks? We deny — we in the pro-choice movement, and in the abortion industry, deny that there is anything like post-abortion syndrome. Yet, it is real, and they do come back, and I couldn't deny their presence. And their numbers were increasing. And I kept asking, why?

Judy Fetrow also worked at a Planned Parenthood abortion clinic. She saw not only the problems of traumatic aftermath, but also the harmfulness of the rationalizations used:

> I often saw women who had been injured emotionally by abortion. However, my supervisor told me, 'If she's having a problem after her abortion, it's because she was having a problem before her abortion.' This was a philosophy that I could not support. Additionally, I could not reconcile that statement with the post-abortion counselling brochure that we had in each counselling room. It struck me that blaming the woman, making the emotional aftermath her fault, was perilously close to what batterers do to victims. We at Planned Parenthood cared for women so much that we only charged 295 dollars for 12 post-abortion counselling sessions. This is more than we charged for an abortion, and it is an amount that is not readily accessible to most of Planned Parenthood's clients.
>
> The saddest emotional complications of abortion are the young women who come back for repeat abortions. These are young women that are still hurting from their first abortion, and their pain has never been addressed by Planned Parenthood. Even clinic workers judge these women harshly. However, repeat abortion is what Alice Miller calls the 'repetition compulsion'. It is continually

repeating the same truama, hoping for a different outcome. But the outcome is always the same.[10]

'Post Abortion Syndrome' is a term that suggests the emotional impact of abortion on many women could be a form of Post-Traumatic Stress Disorder, the modern psychiatric term for 'shell shock' or battle fatigue. Naturally, abortion defenders believe this to be ludicrous. It implies abortion is actually more violent than they claim, and certainly less beneficial to women then they claim. Therefore, they have vociferously argued that it is a myth, merely anti-abortion propaganda.

As with breast cancer, the definitive, unassailable study remains to be done. US Surgeon General Everett Koop investigated this, and that was his conclusion. Abortion defenders immediately trumpeted his findings as proof that the syndrome did not exist, but that was not what he said. What he found was that, though the number of studies is extensive, there was a high correlation between the findings of the studies and the bias of the researchers, for both sides. Too much of the material is anecdotal, or shallow questionnaires done on biased samples (those women who showed up for their follow-up exams). Once again, women do not get unassailable answers on this point, either because this is contrary to the interests of the abortion business, or because a widespread problem that affects only women is not regarded as sufficiently important to expend resources upon. But the anecdotal evidence is remarkably voluminous.

Another aspect of abortion is the psychological impact on those that perform abortions. Nurses see foetal remains very frequently and the doctors not infrequently: that is to say, they see tiny human body parts of organisms that were once alive before they dismembered them. If evidence of Post-Truamatic Stress Disorder cannot be found among the staff which actually perform abortions, then the case is strengthened that pregnancy termination is either not killing, or is 'minor' killing. Can such evidence be found?

Studies of large numbers of abortion staff are rare in scholarly literature. The conclusions of two of them are:

> Obsessional thinking about abortion, depression, fatigue, anger, lowered self esteem, and identity conflicts were prominent. The symptom complex was considered 'transient reactive disorder', similar to 'combat fatigue'.
>
> Ambivalent periods were characterized by a variety of otherwise uncharacteristic feelings and behaviour including withdrawal from colleagues, resistance to going to work, lack of energy, impatience with clients and overall sense of uneasiness. Nightmares, images that could not be shaken and preoccupation were commonly reported. Also common was the deep and lonely privacy within which practitioners had grappled with their ambivalence.[12]

Both studies were made by authors who favour the availability of abortion. The purpose of their studies was to suggest interventions in order to keep abortion staff working. They saw the negative emotions as a threat to abortion accessibility, which they regarded as a social good. Their biases should have countered their actual findings, and those findings surprised them.

Are there studies that counter these findings? I have been unable to find any. In addition to these two large studies, there are some smaller ones and some anecdotal evidence, both from those still performing abortions and those that have stopped. Especially common is a mention of bad dreams related to the work: the vast majority of any discussion of negative emotions include this symptom.

There is a social question as to whether we should expect such misery in people to maintain abortion availability. But this question also goes back full circle: do women really wish to be placing their bodies in the hands of such traumatised people who will be practising surgery on them, especially when other symptoms include edginess, feeling detached from people, and alchohol or drug use?

Judith Fetrow tells us:

> When I started at Planned Parenthood, I saw two types of women working at the clinic. One group were women who had found some way to deal with the emotional and spiritual toll of working with abortion. The second group were women who had closed themselves off emotionally. They were the walking wounded. You could look in their eyes, and see that they were emotionally dead. Unavailable for themselves, or for anyone else.

THE CULTURE

Abortion has affected not just those who procure or provide them. Women who miscarry have long been told to take a long, hot bath and forget about it – they can always have another child. Modern health professionals understand that women need to be allowed to grieve. Yet if intentionally terminating a pregnancy is to be regarded as a right, then what is lost in a miscarriage must be disparaged, causing further pain to women already devastated by such a loss.

One argument held vociferously is that we need abortion for the benefit of children. We can prevent abuse of unwanted children because only wanted children remain. We can lower the violent crime rate because those frustrated children who grow up to commit crimes have not been born. Children that are born are wanted by their parents, and are therefore a well-adjusted generation. But those who argue this simply fail to notice that it does not work that way. Child abuse and crime among the young have soared. Establishing in social policy the notion that it is acceptable to get rid of the inconvenient might actually increase child abuse, by removing the taboo against hurting children. And would being 'wanted' help children? Children should not be expected to meet a standard of being 'wanted' in order to have value. Being overwanted can lead to high expectations that children cannot always achieve, which can lead to abuse. As for the crime rate, the principle of using violence to solve problems is not a good message to be putting out if its reduction is desired.

THE INSULT

The customary right-to-life argument will showcase the wonders of foetal development and then plead for the lives of the unborn children. When asked about the hard cases involving rape or incest the reply will be that, even when so difficult, the same principle applies: the child is innocent.

The feminist pro-abortion will follow this logic backwards. Having identified the injustices that push women into acts of desperation, decried the accommodation of those injustices, expressed the neccessity of changing the underlying causes, the question changes. Suppose a woman has all the social support she needs, the father is taking equal responsibility, and the workplace or school is supportive. Yet she still wants an abortion. Who are you to tell her she can't?

The tenet of feminism is that being human, a living organism of the species homo sapiens, entitles that being to certain basic rights, regardless of gender or other criteria. If we discriminate against any class of human beings, placing them outside the realm of legal protection, then we dynamite the very foundation of feminism. We endanger our own demands for equal rights.

But it goes much deeper than this. The attitude that places pregnancy termination as a 'right' has led to attitudes toxic to the feminist cause. Promoting abortion as necessary for women's equality implies that women require surgery to achieve equality with men, that the whole premise of male domination, women's biological inferiority, is correct. Rather than questioning the premise, it accepts it but draws a different conclusion: this inherent inferiority can be technologically fixed.

Feminism has made a point of viewing the female body positively. Menstrution and menopause are natural and not to be disparaged. Breast-feeding allows the breasts to function for what they were designed for, and should not be publicly discouraged. We should not be expected to make our bodies conform to unrealistic (usually male-orientated) ideals. We are entitled to dignity in our bodies.

What happens, then, when the natural occurrence of an unexpected pregnancy is viewed so negatively? If a 'wanted' pregnancy is healthy, but an 'unwanted' pregnancy is tantamount to a disease, then basic female biology is held in contempt. Feminists broke ground in the early 1970s by taking the disease status assigned to it by male doctors out of pregnancy, yet reassigned that status to 'unwanted' pregnancy. With abortion as 'treatment', normal pregnancy was allowed once more to be seen as possibly pathological, thereby connecting a distaste with pregnancy to a general loathing of the female body. Abortion advocacy has once more sabotaged an important feminist goal.

THE CONTROVERSY

Abortion advocacy is subject to many contradictions. People who assert that women's voices must be listened to nevertheless announce that all women feel one way about 'reproductive rights", belittling women whose opinion differs. Feminists who insist on sisterhood censor their sisters, over and over again. These contradictions would not exist if abortion defenders were confident in their views. Belligerency and proselytizing are common human responses to a tension caused by contradictions in thoughts. People want to sense that their beliefs are internally consistent, and it is stressful to be offered evidence that they are not.

Many are very uncomfortable with abortion, yet also uncomfortable with banning it. Most people wish the whole problem would just go away. The image of the torn apart child weighs heavily on people's minds. Counterbalancing this is the idea that a woman has a right to control the course of her own destiny, and that this is more important than the right to life of a being not fully developed. Ignoring that image of the child is done with the idea that it benefits the woman carrying the child.

But it is not normal or healthy for a woman to want the death of her own child. If she does, then that is a clear sign that injustice has been perpetrated against her. The basic premise of abortion advocacy pits mothers and children against one another. The pro-life feminist asserts that any wedge put between mother and child originates in male dominance, and that no woman really benefits from being alienated from her own body and her own child. There should not be a conflict between women and unborn children. The rights of both must be asserted against a society that is cruel to both. Women do not need our children to be scapegoats for injustice. What we need is justice. The more justice and equality women have, the more the abortion rate will plummet. Abortion serves as an obstacle against those goals, but those goals also serve as the best possible deterrents for abortion.

Once people realize that the best way to relieve the contradiction between caring for tiny children and caring for grown women is to care for them both, then society will be able to work its way out of the current raging controversy. It is in pro-life feminism that the resolution to the current 'abortion wars' lies.

NOTES

1 'Woman wants files opened in 1973 ruling on abortion', by Gayle White, *Atlanta Journal*, 13 December 1988.
2 The *Roe v. Wade* ruling came too late for Norma to abort, and the baby was adopted. Norma recently turned away from the abortion rights cause, proclaiming, 'I have always been pro-life.

I just didn't know it' (Book Reviews, *Studies in Pro-life Feminism* vol. 1 no. 4, Fall 1995, page 78).

3 *Sisterlife* vol XIII, no. 1, Winter 1993.
4 Affidavit, *The State of South Carolina v. Jesse Floyd*, Case no. 30159. He was indited, but never convicted as the case was not pursued.
5 'Back-alley Abortions still here for the Poorest among Us', *Ms Magazine*, May/June 1993.
6 Patricia G. Miller, *The Worst of Times* (Harper Collins, New York 1993), 147.
7 Tisdale, S.,'We do Abortions Here: A Nurse's Story', *Harper's Magazine*, October 1987.
8 'Abortion providers Share Inner Conflicts', Diane M. Gianelli, *American Medical News*, 12 July 1993.
9 'Doctor Warns of Negative Psychological Impact of Sonography in Abortion', *ObGyn News*, 15–28 February 1986.
10 Appleton and Fetrow's remarks come from an audiotape of a conference, 'Meet the Abortion providers III', available from the Pro-Life Action League in Chicago, Illinois.
11 Such-Baer, M., 'Professional Staff Reaction to Abortion Work', *Social Casework*, July 1974).
12 Roe, K.M., 'Private troubles and public issues, providing abortion amid competing definitions', *Social Science and Medicine* 1989, vol. 29, no. 1, 1197.

8

Alternatives to Abortion and Hard Cases

PATRICIA CASEY

ADOPTION

Adoption is out of fashion and has been waning in popularity for over 20 years. In the US, for example, an all-time peak for legal adoptions was reached in 1970, with 89,000, and although federal government ceased compiling national statistics on adoption 1975, there is a belief that the numbers have declined. In Ireland, figures for adoption have been compiled since 1952. In 1994 there were 224 orders made in respect of non-familial adoptions whilst in Britain 6,239 adoption orders were made (separate figures for no-familial adoptions are unavailable), of which only 359 were for children under one year. These figures are startling when placed alongside the figures for abortion from these three countries. In the US one million abortions are performed each year. In 1995, 172, 000 abortions were performed in Britain, and approximately 5,000 women travel from Ireland each year to avail of the practice there.

Surprisingly, adoption is rarely discussed in feminist literature, a lacuna which instead has been filled with pro-choice rhetoric. Why the language of choice should encompass abortion only and not also extend to adoption is an issue which has not been explored, nor have the reasons for the unpopularity of adoption, although I will attempt to open debate on the latter in this chapter.

Neuberger's comment in relation to choice is apposite:

> Why should it be acceptable, in feminist terms, to get rid of an unwanted baby because one is in control of one' s own body and not acceptable to use that body to have a baby and give away to someone else . . . by adoption?[1]

Until the 1970s unmarried women who were pregnant placed their babies for adoption rather than endure the poverty of single motherhood or the institutional opprobrium of society. In addition, adoption was regarded as providing the answer for childless couples to fulfil their understandable need for children. Not only did adoption provide a practical solution to practical needs but it also saved women from the harsh judgement of the community which castigated both the bearers of 'illegitimate' children as well as the children themselves.

Until the 1960s giving birth outside marriage was heavily criticized. A woman was regarded as having 'let herself down', as well as her family, and many entered unsatisfactory marriages rather than endure social opprobrium. This applied as much in Britain and the US as in Ireland. The stigma of single motherhood was such that 'the sins of the father were visited on the child' and an illegitimate child could not be ordained to the Catholic priesthood. The choice for women lay between having the baby adopted or getting married. The gravity of being an unmarried parent was considered greater for women than men since women were viewed as capable of exercising greater sexual control. This served to excuse men whilst blaming women. Thus there were unmarried mothers but no unmarried fathers.

The suffering of many women entering unsatisfactory marriages due to pregnancy is well documented. Such was the stigma of single parenthood that many women chose this unhappy path. Others made their babies available for adoption although this too was traumatic and often clumsily handled.

The procedure for placing a child for adoption has changed irrevocably since the 1960s. Prior to that time images of orphanages, workhouses for unmarried mothers and the forced removal of children abound. Women were not prepared for the loss of their baby immediately after birth, having no contact unless the child chose to re-establish a relationship in later life, an occurrence which was rarely discussed nor considered. Subsequently, if marriage occurred, a woman's husband was often unaware of her earlier pregnancy and its conclusion; hence the return of a long-lost child was a cause of sadness and an event not to be contemplated. The child would certainly have been denied information about parentage until adolescence. This was not for any malicious reason but in the belief that such children, for their own stability, should believe that they were the natural children of their adoptive parents. The grotesque practice of trying to match the likeness of adoptive parents to child was common. Records were not diligently kept since tracing was not an issue for consideration at the outset. Even when contact was made, the birth mother often rejected this, having buried her own sorrow and concealed her trauma even from family members. Recognition of the suffering of both natural mothers and their offspring lead to a perception that the institutional procedures of adoption were cruel and ill-served its recipients.

The reality of the adoption procedures had changed greatly by the 1980s and had outpaced the perception. Unfortunately the two have not become realigned. While orphanages, grief and loss dominated popular descriptions of adoption, women contemplating making their babies available for adoption were prepared for the loss of the baby, given time and space to make their decision and encouraged to write as well as articulate their feelings. They had regular contact with their infants until adoption took place and were encouraged to meet the prospective adoptive parents. Following adoption, they were provided with regular reports on the child's progress and, through social services, remained in contact with the adoptive parents, making eventual reunification easier and less

emotionally disturbing. However, by the time this modern procedure was insti-
tuted the press, popular magazines and feminist thinking were unwilling or
unable to change the negativity surrounding adoption.

Many sad tales about the cruel handling of adoptions in the 50s and 60s has
contributed to the mistaken belief that such procedures are still implemented.
An archivist in Dublin recently revealed that many hundreds of babies in the
1960s were given false passports and sent to the US to be adopted. Many such
children have come forwards as adults to confirm this. There has been no
suggestion that their lives were unhappy or non-productive – just that they are
sad and without an identity. But it is illogical to demonize all adoptions in the
face of radical changes that now ensure sensitivity and openness.

Mothers making their children available for adoption are popularly viewed as
passive agents faced with authoritarian bureaucracy while the children are cast
as victims without identity, further reinforcing established prejudices against
adoption. The historical proximity between hasty marriages and the frequent
recourse to adoption has contributed to the negative mental set where adoption
is concerned. These popular images are a travesty on the truth – figures from
the US suggest women placing their children for adoption are not the most
disadvantaged. They are less likely to be receiving welfare assistance, more likely
to have college-educated parents and more likely to have completed high-school
education, than single women who keep their babies.[2]

A recent novel about two girls' obsessive search for their mothers who
abandoned them exemplifies the victim status of adoptive children. Notions of
the superiority of biology over parenting, nature over nurture, dominate this tale,
giving credence to the notion that a child without a biological backdrop is
damaged.[3] Rosalind Miles points to the error of this, commenting, 'adopted
children strongly disliked repeated overt reference to their situation by outside
agencies and its implications'. She quotes Dr Alexina McWhinnie, an expert in
adoption from Dundee University: 'It is like planting a tree and then digging it
up all the time to see if it had taken.'[4]

Many women say 'I could never give up my child', yet are willing to abort
their unborn with little awareness of the nature of this act. Ignorance of the
finality of this decision, coupled with the notion that adoption is traumatic for
both mother and child while abortion is not has lead to a 'poor press' for adoption
and militated against it as an issue for consideration. In Ireland, 15% of children
are 'non-marital'. In Britain the figure is 30%.

Adoption is seldom discussed except occasionally and fleetingly during pre-
abortion counselling sessions. In Ireland, under the terms of the Abortion
Information Act (1995) it is compulsory to discuss alternatives to abortion whilst
being illegal to promote abortion. But this pro-active approach has not increased
the numbers of children for adoption. The attachment of stigma has reverted
from single parenthood to adoption. A similar lack of enthusiasm for adoption
is evident in Britain where it is mentioned as an afterthought when dealing with

an unplanned pregnancy. Such is the antipathy to adoption that a gynaecologist who runs an abortion clinic in London recently stated, '. . . It is not in any way standard to offer advice on adoption. It would be subversive . . . In fact I would consider firing anyone who did this.'[5] A National Health Service spokesperson confirmed that this contravenes recently issued guidelines which specify that advice and information on adoption should be provided.

Many pregnant women considering placing their children for adoption are deterred from this course by their belief that they will have no further contact with their child unless in some unspecified time in the future when s/he seeks them out. Others worry that they will never be able to rebuild their lives, fearing that an unknown child will return. Many fear their child will be damaged by the separation. But reassurance about these concerns can be found since mothers may keep in contact with their child's progress whilst preserving their anonymity. Concerns about tracing can also be allayed since face to face contact is only made with the permission of the birth mother.

Adoption is an issue which should concern all child-bearing women, but should have a special resonance for feminists, who have long been concerned that nurturing and caring has been overpowered by what is aggressive, overbearing and masculine in patriarchal societies. This thesis is fundamental to the feminist ideology. Nowhere is the opportunity to nurture and care more evident than in the woman's decision to complete a pregnancy, to give life in the face of adversity — a decision to end the life of an unborn child is the very antithesis of the ideals that inspired the founders of feminism.

HARD CASES

The right to life is the one right which is a precondition for the establishment of all other rights. It is a truism, but nonetheless important, to state that without life we do not exist, hence its centrality in considering all other rights. In discussing rights it is necessary to examine the basis on which rights are removed or established — ordinarily the onus is on those who would expunge a right, to demonstrate why that right should be removed. Following from this it is pertinent to pose the question: 'What is the morally relevant distinction between the foetus before birth and a child after birth such that we say that one has a right to life and the other doesn't?'[6] It is on this basis that this discussion of abortion in 'hard cases' will proceed, although due to restriction on space only rape, disability and suicide risk as grounds for abortion will be considered.

RAPE

The use of the penis as weapon is acknowledged by many feminists. Nowhere is this more obvious than in the crime of rape. Carrying massive emotional connotations, rape is the most reviled of all crimes against women. When a pregnancy results it is not surprising that many, even those who oppose abortion on principle, believe that in this circumstance it is justified. As with other emotional issues, arguing the contrary is fraught with difficulty and likely to result in vitriolic condemnation. But there are a number of inherent assumptions in this hard case argument that must be challenged. When one examines the justification unfettered by the ideology, the pro-choice arguments are less strong than at first appear.

There is very little research available about the psychological effects of pregnancy on rape victims, and this is hardly surprising given its rarity with the totality of pregnancies. Anecdotal evidence, always unsatisfactory, is available and conforms to predictions that some women adjust to bearing the child, even though the initial emotion was abhorrence, while others reject the child.

It is important to consider the status of the foetus. Are the rights of foetuses conceived by rape different from those conceived in other circumstances? Some argue that when a pregnancy occurs the mother has entered into a contract with the foetus, which a raped woman cannot be said to have done. However, this argument could extend to include pregnancies resulting from contraceptive failure since a woman may not consider she has a contract with this foetus either. Situations in which a mother can be considered to be obligated to the foetus is therefore arbitrary, and could include all unplanned pregnancies. Why, it could be logically argued, should the contract be limited to all except those conceived by rape? It is therefore unconvincing to support a woman's right to abortion following rape only using the contract argument.

The stages of development, and therefore the physical status, of a foetus is the same, whether conceived by rape or otherwise. Supporting abortion in rape cases exclusively suggests that the foetus is less than human and not deserving of the respect accorded to other foetuses. This is clearly an untenable position and has no justification. In order to overcome this position, supporters of abortion in rape cases resort to using language to demonize the foetus, for example, 'a rapist's child', as if the mother were just an incubator, or imply eugenic concerns by asking questions such as 'what sort of child will *he* turn out to be?' This approach serves to displace the hatred for the rapist onto his biological child, blurring the boundary between genitor and progeny. This serves to rob the foetus of any rights that may be usually afforded the unborn. Richards uses the following analogy :

> It would be quite unthinkable to take the life of an adult human being to save a different human being from undeserved unhappiness. Imagine, for instance,

what would be said if anyone tried to kill someone in order to give vital organs to someone else (perhaps a relative) who had been the innocent victim of a criminal attack.[7]

What then is the justification for allowing abortion in cases of rape since the status of the foetus is the same as in cases of non-rape? One argument is that the pregnancy has occurred as a result of coercion and is therefore not desired. The force applied in rape is the aspect which distinguishes it from consensual sex. The woman who is raped has not willingly entered into a sexual relationship with her assailant whilst the woman engaged in consensual sex has given permission although this is often implicit rather than explicit. Sometimes, a woman may consent to sex with reluctance, due to the power relations that may be present in heterosexual relationships.

The giving of permission should imply accepting responsibility for the consequences of an action whilst a result which accrues from coercion can carry no onus of responsibility. Those who would deprive a woman of abortion in these circumstances yet allow it in rape must therefore believe that she must accept responsibility for her action, an action freely entered into albeit with undesirable consequences. As Richards develops this argument she comments:

> The only time when we insist that a particular consequence must follow a particular action and not allow people to try and escape the consequence by their unaided activity, is when the consequence is intended as a punishment.[8]

Richards sees the readiest explanation of a willingness to allow abortions to rape victims but not otherwise as a desire to punish those women who could have prevented their conceptions. The desire to inflict punishment may not be the conscious sub-text of those who support abortion to rape victims only, but it is the inevitable conclusion of the arguments when examined untrammeled by emotion or vitriol. Moreover, the use of the unborn child as the instrument of punishment seems inescapable in the context of this thesis.

Some argue that on compassionate grounds a woman who has suffered as a result of rape should not be forced to continue a pregnancy to term. However, raped pregnant women are sufferers among many other suffering women. It is arguable, but not testable, whether raped pregnant women suffer more than non-raped pregnant women and difficult to justify abortion exclusively for the raped sufferer whilst depriving other suffering women of the same option. Many feminists will not engage in such a debate and argue for abortion in all cases of suffering pregnant women.

A further issue concerns whether the pregnancy or the rape makes the greater contribution to the emotional trauma of a woman, and there is no research to assist us in this. It can be argued that the suffering is not relieved by aborting the foetus — merely that the anger of the woman and society is projected on the foetus without any impact on the underlying trauma from the rape.

If, as some argue, there is a dual suffering inherent in being raped and then carrying the pregnancy to term, the same argument can be made about the dual violation of the woman, firstly by rape, and then by the violence of abortion. The emotional pain associated with either situation cannot be gainsaid and abortion does not 'unrape' a woman or remove the violence that has been perpetrated against her. Thus arguments related to suffering, while superficially appealing, are more complex than at first seem obvious.

DISABILITY

As with rape, many who abhor abortion on demand concede the principle in relation to handicap, supporting its provision when that risk exists. Herein lies one of the problems; that abortion is offered without the certainty of abnormality. Thus, even if one conceded the right to abortion for definitively proven disability, that principle is being transgressed since some 'normal' foetuses will also be included. A proportion of prenatal genetic tests will give false positive results i.e. a foetus is unaffected even though the test result is positive. If abortion were chosen in all of these cases then a significant minority of aborted foetuses would in fact be 'normal'. The impression has been given that an amniocentesis confirms the presence of a genetic abnormality when it is only a screening technique which points to the possibility rather than the certainty of disability. Offering abortion in these circumstances can at best be described as the culling of the foetus on the probability that it may be disabled. Even criminals are given the benefit of the doubt when the evidence is equivocal: and the abandonment of capital punishment reflected society's unease with the imperfections in the system.

Arguments that the provision of genetic screening serve to reassure women are counter-intuitive since they place enormous pressure on women to seek abortion when a positive result is obtained. Some gynaecologists contend that they are not seeking to destroy but to reassure – this has a hollow ring when the figures for abortion following a positive result are examined. In Belfast, for example, in 1995 over 75% of women receiving a positive test result sought abortion.

The basic principle of abortion for disability requires further exploration in relation to the rights of the foetus. Is a disabled foetus less deserving of protection than a 'normal' one? The neonate, whether disabled or not, at least in theory, is entitled to the full protection of the criminal law. This equivalence after birth should make it difficult to argue that prenatally both are not equivalent, notwith-standing the current state of abortion legislation in Europe. Leaving aside legal considerations, the moral question is whether the disabled child, at any time, is as much a human as the able child. If the answer was 'no' then the criteria for establishing this i.e. when a child is no longer to be considered human, would have to be determined. Is it when the child cannot walk? Is it when the child has an IQ of less than 60 or a genetic disorder such as Down's syndrome, haemophilia, homosexuality or colour blindness? Would those with genetic predispositions, in which certain conditions manifest themselves late in life under certain conditions, be included? These questions point to the arbitrariness of assigning full human status to one group of humans while depriving others of that recognition.

In many cultures having a female infant is regarded with the same ambivalence as having a disabled baby in western societies. In order to produce a male heir, many women seek amniocentesis and abortion, if they find they are carrying a female child. The ancient birthing box has been replaced by prenatal genetic testing. The X chromosome is considered a genetic handicap – do the same principles apply in considering abortion for reasons of gender and if not, why not? It is tempting to argue that this is eugenics exceeding itself, yet the principles are the same. For the feminist, they illustrate the issue more cogently than for any other aspect of the eugenic debate.

The motive behind abortion for disability also need to be examined although these are often emotive. One possible spur is the altruism of saving a child from needless suffering. However, the arbiter of the possible effects of that suffering on the child is the doctor and family of the unborn child. In this instance the person most concerned i.e. the child is not afforded the opportunity of choosing whether to accept that suffering. It could be argued that this choice should be conferred on the 'sufferer' herself. Many disabled people attest to their own happiness, or at least degrees of emotional equilibrium equivalent to the 'able-bodied', in the face of what seems to those able-bodied to be unbearable misfortune. It is likely that those justifying abortion on grounds of disability, physical or mental, are projecting their own fears onto the unborn person.

It was Josef Mengele who applied the principle of 'life unworthy of life'. This spectre continues to haunt arguments about abortion of those with handicap. It is worth contemplating whether there is an innate belief underpinning abortion of disabled foetuses that they are not deserving of life, and that society, that is, the exchequer is being saved some cost. Many are uncomfortable when they see disabled people, either staring or avoiding them. Perhaps such misgivings underlie beliefs about abortion for disability and are rationalized as compassion for the person or the parents concerned.

The desire of every woman for a healthy child is understandable but this is quiet different from the notion of the right of every woman to a healthy child. A society which does not care for and protect its vulnerable citizens cannot be described as a compassionate or mature society. The temptation to deny the existence of physical, psychological and intellectual disability by the culling of those so afflicted is as great as when the walled institutions were the repositories of society's unwanted. Regrettably, this temptation still exists. To succumb on the ground of compassion is yet a further contorted defence of an unconscionable practice.

SUICIDE RISK AND THE RIGHT TO ABORTION

This issue is of special interest in Ireland since it was on this basis that the Irish Supreme Court judged that a woman had a right to an abortion. A fourteen-year-old became pregnant as a result of repeated sexual abuse by the father of a school friend. On the basis that she had threatened suicide, the court asserted, with one dissenting judge, that her right to life should be vindicated (by allowing the abortion) and that this was in keeping with the constitutional protection of the unborn inserted in 1983. The introduction of abortion was in the basis of the risk to Ms 'X's life, with suicide being the test. This was an emotional time in Ireland and feelings ran high. The girl had previously been prevented by injunction from travelling to England for an abortion by the then Attorney General.

So, what of the suicide risk as constituting a grounds for abortion? Suicide is always a tragedy, yet, not withstanding the extensive coverage it receives in the media, it is still a rare event. Women have a much lower rate than men and the rate is even lower during pregnancy[9] than at other times in a woman's life. The reasons for this are unknown but the risk for psychiatric illness in general is lower during pregnancy, which itself constitutes a protective factor.

The issue of the status of the foetus is not in question, since those arguing in favour of abortion in these circumstances would contend that it is simply a choice of who's right to life should be vindicated - the mother's or that of her unborn child. This presumes that a risk of suicide exists which can be predicted to occur as a direct result of pregnancy. The prediction of suicide is one of the great challenges to society and one in which we are still deficient. Even for patients deemed to be high-risk, such as those who make attempts by overdosing or self-mutilation, the prediction is abysmally low due to the enormous number of false positives. This means that the numbers predicted to commit suicide using known risk factors greatly exceed the numbers who actually do. The problem of poor prediction stems from the difficulty in forecasting rare events. This is therefore a fundamental flaw in prescribing abortion for suicide risk, in order to prevent a rare event, which is even rarer in the pregnant woman and which itself is of poor predictability.

A further aspect to the prevention of suicide during pregnancy relates to the treatability of suicidality. The most common cause of serious suicidal ideation or intention is depressive illness. This, however, is treatable, even during pregnancy. The array of anti-depressants available nowadays has enhanced the options for treating this disorder. Unless a patient is actively suicidal, treatment can be provided on an out-patient basis. What of the suicidal ideation which can occasionally arise due to the crisis of pregnancy? by definition a crisis is short-lived and there are, and should be, a constellation of psychiatric supports available to women without recourse to the taking of either life. Indeed, those who argue for abortion in this situation would argue against any rash decisions such as marrying the father or having the baby adopted. This same rationale applies when considering abortion; the provision of abortion during a crisis reaction could be deemed to be placing a woman at risk of psychological problems after. The risk of such problems after abortion is at least as high as the prevalence of postnatal depression, irrespective of cultural background.[10]

One risk factor for post-abortion psychological problems is a prior psychiatric history – arguments that the provision of abortion in the context of suicide risk is justified must therefore be recast. Arguments supporting the provision of an intervention to prevent a rare behaviour of low predictability which has a treatable cause, the intervention of which itself might be a risk factor for future psychiatric illness, require a leap of justification of Olympian proportions.

CONCLUSION

The scenarios I have discussed demonstrate that the use of hard cases to support an ideology of legal abortion has very little to do with the health of women's psyches. A feminist reappraisal of such problematic approaches to crisis pregnancies is needed as a matter of urgency.

NOTES

1 Neuberger, J., *Whatever's Happening to Women? Promises, Practices and Pay-Offs* (Kyle Cathie, London, 1991).
2 Colker, R., *Abortion and Dialogue: Pro-life, Pro-choice and American Law* (1992)
3 Forster, M., *Shadow Baby* (Chatto & Windus, London, 1996).
4 Miles, R., *The Children We Deserve* (HarperCollins, London, 1995)
5 Today, BBC Radio 4, 28 August, 1996.
6 Gentles, I. (ed.), *A Time to Choose Life* (Stoddart, Toronto, 1990).
7 Richards, J.R., *The Sceptical Feminist* (Penguin, London, 1980), 270.
8 Ibid., 271.
9 Appleby, L., 'Suicide During Pregnancy and in the First Postnatal Year', *British Medical Journal*, 30, 1991,137–40.
10 Zolese, G. Blacker, C.V.R., 'The Psychological Complications of Therapeutic Abortion', *British Journal of Psychiatry*, 160, 1992, 742–9.

Obstinate Questionings:
An Experience of Abortion

CATHERINE SPENCER

> Those obstinate questionings
> Of sense and outward things,
> Fallings from us, vanishings;
> Blank misgivings of a creature
> Moving about in worlds not realised,
> High instincts before which our mortal nature
> Did tremble like a guilty thing surprised.
>
> Wordsworth, 'Ode on Intimations of Mortality'

I recently saw a film on television about a woman who had shot her three children, one of whom had died, because she was infatuated with a man who did not want to be a father, either of his own or of anyone else's children. In the protracted trial scene, the prosecuting lawyer depicts the crime in lurid detail, and the camera cuts, Hollywood fashion, to the faces of the jury – good, honest American citizens, appalled by the depravity of a woman who could kill her own children. In a later exchange between the lawyer and his wife, she cries, 'How could she? How could any woman do that? Women have a primal instinct to protect their children – children are their future.' Her husband shakes his head, unable to explain. The woman is of course found guilty, and, in sentencing her to the longest prison term possible, the judge declares solemnly that the death of a child is the most terrible of all losses and that when that death is intentionally caused its horror cannot be adequately expressed.

One-dimensional and overblown as the film was, it had particular resonance for me: I am a woman who had an abortion after intense pressure from my partner. In other words, there was an unborn child – or, if that word seems too emotive, too shocking, a potential child – and the parents of that child or potential child took a decision for it to die. It is not that simple or neat, of course: our motivations were complex and various and reached back to the recesses of our own childhoods (although we were hardly conscious of that then), and I was not, as my statement implies, an innocent bystander of what happened. I shared, *ipso facto*, in the responsibility for it. As I watched the film, I felt the resurgence of the old guilt (generally manageable now, through my long dissection of and reflection on it), the old feelings of self-horror at what I did, or allowed to happen. I felt exactly like a mother who has killed her own child – appalled, confused, remorseful. As I write, the 'understanding' and the rationalizations are back in place and I once more feel the compassion for myself that I have trained myself to feel. Yet somewhere within, beyond the reach of my rational mind, the sense of horror continues unabated and is apt to re-surface.

What needs to be said at the outset is that I do not consider myself to be in anyone's 'pay'. I speak on behalf of no one but myself and, perhaps, of women who have been through the same experience with the same consequences. There is, for me, no church or cause into which I hope my words will recruit members (although I am not entirely without ulterior motive, for do I not hope that my sense of my experience will be understood and acknowledged by others?) and I have not been so suffocated by guilt and grief that I can no longer see the truly daunting complexities and ambiguities of the subject. I know that, in what might be called our post-feminist society, abortion is now widely seen solely as an issue of women's rights; indeed, that notion is so well-entrenched in our cultural norms that to oppose abortion seems to many people a fundamental opposition to women's emancipation. I know that we live in a relativist age in which people who hold to absolute values are generally viewed (at least sometimes not without cause) with suspicion or derision. Finally, as a woman who has suffered from abortion, I know that my suffering is in a sense convenient to some people's 'campaigns' and liable to be exploited by them, with varying degrees of consciousness or cynicism.

The post-abortion territory is a bleak place, peopled by ghostly figures mouthing slogans that cannot revive the deadness of heart that one feels. I do not mean to impugn the sincerity or integrity of all these campaigners and, indeed, those on the pro-life side of the fence raise questions about abortion and detail its consequences in a way that my experience has confirmed – yet their campaigning cannot contain the heart of the matter for me. It is the truth and authenticity of my own experience that I seek to enter, nothing else; of course, the campaigns of women and others before me made my abortion possible and the campaigns of those who defend life at all costs sought to prevent it, but in a curious sense they seem not to have great bearing upon it. Perhaps one of my most agonized and private questions – and one that would negate this whole piece – is whether one can legislate against human folly and whether I might not have been driven by what is termed love to betray myself and my child even had abortion been illegal. (Before – because my life seems irretrievably and absolutely divided into 'before' and 'after' – I was no lover of ideologies or extreme positions and my experience has not changed that. If anything it has deepened it, for now I understand more intimately how ideals can crumble in the face of emotional realities.)

For a time I chose to override this innate uneasiness with movements and campaigns: overwhelmed by my grief, I sought refuge in a pro-life group. They were, quite properly, interested in promoting their belief that the taking of unborn life is wrong. I was interested in my own lost child, trying hopelessly and unconsciously to fill the void that he or she had left and to atone for the wrong my heart —if not my head —told me had been done. But as I began to understand more of the processes of this pain, I realized that I was essentially justifying my own experience by adorning it with others' ideological beliefs, just as some women use the language of the pro-choice movement to bolster up theirs. But now I seek the freedom to ask questions, not to hang others' answers on me like so many borrowed rags. And the questions that any woman who seeks fully to understand her abortion experience asks are, perforce, enormous; the experience can be so awesome in its depth and duration that she also attempts to control and contain it with rational understanding.

The first, perhaps the overriding, such question must concern the ethics of abortion. Whatever some 'pro-choicers' may say, abortion is a matter of life or death and it simply cannot be lightly dismissed. At this moment, after such deep and long reflection that it makes the speed of my original decision seem utterly absurd and tragic, I feel I am not in possession of absolute answers. I had always wanted children and when I discovered I was pregnant I felt what I can only describe as waves of extraordinary and unconditional love for the baby —I use this word not to prove some point of science or dogma but merely to convey the sense of relatedness that I had —but when the man whom I thought I loved (and to the shame of having participated in the death of my own child is added the shame of having loved a man who could behave in such a way) urged me to have an abortion, I felt quite unable to cope with a child alone. I felt terrified of the responsibility of bringing into the world one whose birth was so unwelcome to all but its mother. I can see that some would say that those facts change everything. Why should I, because I was not courageous and independent enough to choose what I really wanted and because I have suffered such severe consequences from my own weakness, seek to prevent other women from obtaining what they really want and what is, they say, their right?

It is a fair question, as far as it goes. But I don't think it goes very far. To say that a woman has a 'right' to an abortion simply because she desires it seems to me morally flimsy. If something is a right merely because I desire it, then do I not have a right to rob a bank if I want? Well, the obvious rejoinder comes, we do not have a right to our desires if they violate someone else's. And there of course is the heart of the matter for so many people: is or is not a foetus a 'someone' whose rights can be violated by its destruction? I am a reasonably intelligent, reasonably educated person, but I cannot possibly make an authoritative pronouncement on that —I doubt that I could do so even after decades of reflection; I could give an opinion, of course, but that is hardly the same as the definitive statement of the truth. What is certain is that the foetus cannot express what it does or does not want and so cannot object to its fate. Does that justify our imposing our values upon it, even if we make the questionable assumption that women who have abortions are implacably 'opposed' to the foetus? That seems uncomfortably close to the traditionally male use of oppression by force: the stronger shall dominate the weaker, the bigger the smaller, the richer the poorer, the voiced the voiceless. Many 'pro-choicers' get embroiled in such unwitting contradictions; what they condone in one situation, they condemn in another. I do not accuse them of hypocrisy so much as lack of reflection.

Some 'pro-lifers' speak of foetal pain. Is abortion a terrifying experience for a foetus? I do not really attach much importance to the possibility, perhaps because to do so would be more than I can bear. On the other hand, I cannot, and do not seek to, deny that what was destroyed was a human life, with a universe of talents and desires, a whole destiny and series of meanings lying within it, as the oak lies within the acorn —and the implications of that are enormous. Because my child was not born, his or her children would never be born: who would they have been? What dreams would they now never have, what tales would they never now spin? Such language may sound purple-tinged, yet it does not do justice to the depth of the longing I feel and have felt to go back and choose again, to give birth to this unique individual who was both part of me and separate from me. Such a loss of 'all that should have been' and such grief are of course known to anyone who experiences an untimely bereavement but, again, they have a particularly agonized, perhaps even pathological, edge in abortion – because things did not have to be this way, because one 'chose' the loss.

Yet this emotional distress does not quite square with my reasoning, imperfect as it is, about the ethics of what I did. As a writer friend, someone used to observing the vagaries and dualities of human nature, perceptively remarked, the most vivid and painful dilemmas are not between right and wrong but between right and right. Or, in this case, between wrong and wrong. Why did I, who felt deep and genuine love for the burgeoning life inside me and who felt that life did indeed have some sacred, miraculous quality, allow something that I felt be so wrong to happen? Because the alternative, at that time and in that state – although I would hardly say that my so-called decision making occurred in circumstances conducive to wise, calm reflection –seemed to me more wrong: to bring into the world a child who would have an unwilling and absent father. My parents had acrimoniously divorced when I was quite young and I knew the peculiarly bitter and lonely taste of the longing for a united, loving family that could never be fulfilled. There are still times when I do not truly know whether I did the wronger thing or the righter thing – and I do not know whether I do not know that because the culpability of having participated in the death of my own child is more than my psyche can assume, so that I need, come what may, to find the get-out clause that lets me off the hook. I truly do not know. I do not know beyond all doubt that a life of suffering, or some suffering, is better than no life at all. Would life have been so terrible for my child? Did I justly allow her[1] to sleep in the white blanket of nothingness, of not-life? If she had a voice, if somehow she could have expressed a preference when she was without language or thought, what would she have said? How could I possibly claim with certainty that she would have wished for life, no matter what the nature or quality of that life? On the other hand, how could I possibly presume to know that she would not have wanted it? Is there not, as I have tried to show, something suspect about basing our actions solely on desire? How can I know for sure? How can anyone know? The only fact that seems certain is that there was life and then there was not and that the destruction of that life has caused such agonized and grief-stricken questions - questions that I can never fully answer.

And then, how do we truly know whether the 'right to life' takes precedence over the 'right to choose' or vice versa? How do we know whether something is a right? Who assigns it to us, how do we know it is ours? Someone once commented to me that it would be more useful to talk not of the right to life but of the power of life. And that is the closest I have come to understanding the depth of my questions and to formulating something like a response; for some, that power of life is a religious concept, but I am not concerned to amplify that. I believe that we must find our own spiritual understanding – something that, in any case, we all do, whether we see it like that or not. The power of life can be observed without being named or categorized. One might reach the conclusion, as I did, having weighed all the evidence in the balance – as I did not – that the taking of a life in a given situation is the lesser of two evils, but the power of life is so commanding that (if one is sensitive to it) one never truly believes that. One remains forever after in a state of limbo in which the heart is not convinced by the reasoning of the head and cries out for satisfaction, cries to be given what was brutally taken from it. The power of life is such that one regrets its destruction far more readily than one regrets its existence. What exists is simply itself; one cannot imagine what life would be like if it were not but it fills the space of such imaginings, making them essentially irrelevant. It is difficult, perhaps impossible, accurately to describe the hellishness of what was but was never known.

And then the pendulum swings again. The 'on the other hands', the attempts to fill the void. Because life seemed sacred to me, the quality of it seemed sacred also. One, at least, of my motivations was a wish to protect my child, in the best way that my society seemed to present at that time. And that is the cry of many who favour abortion principally on the ground of compassion rather than of a woman's right to determine whether or not she should have a child. People who care about children care that they might be abused or mistreated; how tempting to say that if a child is unwanted, far better it should not be born, only to suffer rejection and insecurity. But I have come to understand that the correlation between 'wantedness' and ill-treatment is problematic; so much can change over the course of a pregnancy, for one thing, that what was initially a crisis and a problem can transform into a much-loved baby. And, critically, I now believe that the availability of abortion itself contributes to this phenomenon of unwanted-ness. People who might otherwise have rallied round and given support that is indeed very necessary, can withdraw, as can the mother, and see abortion as the answer. If a so-called crisis pregnancy were viewed not as a problem but as an unexpected gift, would that not in itself change people's attitudes, enable them to cope? I might not choose to ally myself with some pro-life campaigners but I must ally myself with some of their questions. Can the legitimization of the destruction of unborn children help to foster the care and protection of born children? It is a strange, almost nightmarish logic that could argue that. Gitta Sereny[2] makes the point, in regard to the Nazis' eugenic programme, that 'a licence to kill creates a momentum which defies moral sensibility and discernment and destroys the capacity of the individual to distinguish between good and evil or, and this is perhaps even worse, to act against a recognized wrong.' I know this is the sort of thing, albeit less sensitively expressed, that extreme pro-lifers might say and yet, again, I can only testify to the truth of it from my own experience. Legalizing an act that the sensitive human psyche actually knows to be abhorrent blunts the moral organism and plunges it into deep confusion. It is probably why I do not know whether what I did was ethically right or wrong, why the hearings that I daily conduct into my own case are unlikely ever to reach an unequivocal verdict.

Another reason for this inability to locate such certainties after abortion is the gap that exists between what society says one should feel (and what some women do indeed claim to feel or rather not to feel) and what one actually experiences. The reactions of many, perhaps most, people – of good, honest citizens – to my abortion, and to abortion generally, are so dissimilar to their reactions at the intentional destruction of a born child that one might imagine that something else entirely were involved, that before a child is born it bears no relation to its future human self and, in the early stages, does not even exist. As though a pregnant woman became a mother only when she has been pregnant for a certain amount of time – when, perhaps, the child can exist independently of the woman. In other words, there must be a moment at which the foetus becomes a child and the inhuman the human; at what hour, minute and second does this occur? Who can determine it, and by what authority? This bizarre mincing of time is coupled with the central distinction of 'wantedness': if a woman wants her unborn child and she loses it, grief is legitimate – although the loss of miscarriage is still imperfectly understood and accepted – but if she apparently ('apparently' being the key to so much inner ambiguity and distress) does not want it and seeks an abortion, she dispenses with the necessity for grieving. Can nature, and millennia of human evolution and genetic memory, be tricked into submission by the exercise of personal preference, and the shock of the massive biological and psychological change of pregnancy overcome by talk of rights and choices? Are we so truly master and mistress of all we survey?

Is it merely our lack of imagination, that cannot pierce the darkness of a woman's womb, that puts abortion into such a different category from the death of born and visible life? Or is it because we have not, through fear of seeming politically correct or hopelessly conservative, sufficiently questioned the stock feminist line that abortion gives women independence from the tyranny of their bodies, their base nature, allowing them freedom to rise to the heights of men? Is not the fact that I and a significant number of others that I have known or read about can testify that abortion was for us an imprisonment rather than a liberation reason enough to question it? If the so-called – and glorified – choice is flawed by lack of understanding and information and if women are so constituted that they bond, instinctively and powerfully, to the growing foetus in their womb so that their very being is cut by the loss of the foetus, should we not maybe begin to re-think the whole thing? The answer, at the risk of sounding self-pitying, is that few people seem to think so. Yet to deny that women have naturally maternal feelings because that would somehow diminish them, make them less than men, is again to think in a strangely patriarchal way; it is to honour traditionally male values of what might be called brute autonomy and to demean those of nurturing and tenderness.

Were it possible for me to go back and 'choose' again, in the knowledge of all that would befall me subsequently, I should choose differently and have my baby. In the light of my own understanding of the issue, that choice would therefore be a primarily selfish one. The point is, of course, that with the knowledge that I now have I would have a degree of choice that I had not then, in my ignorance and fear. And I have heard that same story of ignorance and fear many times; it is important to say that there are women for whom the free exercise of their 'rights' simply was not on the agenda. They did not choose abortion but submitted to it in vulnerability and desperation. Such choicelessness is seen, of course, as the woman's 'right' and no-one else's concern. Even those who see abortion clinics as the Valhalla of feminist' heroines admit the frequent lack of real choice in abortion. Chalker and Downes' book, hailed by one feminist as 'perhaps the most important book ever written on women's rights and women's lives', describes how a young woman who already had a two-year-old child decided to have an abortion, telling the counsellor, 'This is my decision, but it is not my choice.'[3] The championing of such stoic fatalism and resignation before difficulties that are surely not insurmountable is surprising for a movement that has 'choice' and 'freedom' as its watchwords; what if that young woman had had greater financial resources, what if there were greater societal support for children and mothers, what if she had been enabled to have her choice rather than her decision? What if there might be options other than between the devil and the deep blue sea?

The arguments I have so far covered all emerged out of the original question about whether abortion is right or wrong. I suspect that most people fall into the trap of answering that question in the light of their own experiences or beliefs, and I am no exception to that. Yet I doubt that such subjectivity can illuminate the whole – to that degree, at least, I am not a relativist. Truth, while rarely pure and never simple, as Wilde joked, must nonetheless surely have a more universal quality. For every woman who feels as I feel there is another who maintains that she suffered no lasting damage from abortion, although she may have experienced short-term sadness or sense of loss, that it was the right decision for her and that she had the right to make that right decision. It is interesting to note as an aside, however, that few women who have had what one might call a positive experience of abortion talk openly about it; since it was in their eyes so positive, what is the root of their silence about it? If they feel no shame, why do they too subscribe to the almost universal taboo on the subject?

One friend among several who claim that abortion did not pose an ethical or emotional problem to them stands out particularly in my mind. She and her boyfriend, who were in love, married because she was pregnant; she wanted the child but her boyfriend was in any case dead set against abortion. I knew this because my friend had been with me in moments of my grief and self-torment, and we had discussed abortion quite freely.

The child turned out to be children, twins. Not long after their birth, my friend and her family moved north and our contact was broken. Then, about a year later, I received a letter from her; she told me that she had recently had an abortion —or 'termination' as she called it, perhaps unable to use the more brutal, clinical word. The twins were still babies, emotional and financial resources were tightly stretched and they (what had happened to her husband's abhorrence of abortion? Presumably the same as had happened to my own sense of the sanctity and the wonder of life when faced with the circumstances that made life seem no longer blessed but full of terror and uncertainty) had felt it was in everyone's best interests if she had an abortion. She said that she knew that it was the right thing to have done and that she had felt not a moment's regret. Something in her insistence on this and in her justification of abortion in general —arguments that she had not voiced before, although that might have been in deference to my own feelings —made me suspect that all was not as clear and simple as she wanted it to be. However, it was plain that she did not want the child and she maintained that it was her right not to have it. What could I say? Was this my friend, generous and sensitive as I knew her to be, saying that she had no feeling for a life that bore such an intimate connection to herself, no longing to see and hold it, no grief at its death? Our reactions were such polar opposites that I felt it would be impossible for us to communicate, but I wrote her a long and heartfelt reply. I was not surprised that I did not receive a reply; I took her silence to mean that she, too, felt that the differences between us were irreconcilable.

The fact that I and other women have suffered deeply from abortion is simply —though vitally —an argument for real counselling before such a drastic and irreversible step is undertaken so that women who are ambivalent or likely to be unable to cope with the reality or the ramifications of abortion are fully informed about, and supported in, other options. It is an argument for telling more of the truth about what abortion can be, for piercing through the hackneyed rhetoric about abortion being a woman's right. And here more questions arise. Why are feminists not concerned about this damage to women, why are the voices of women such as me drowned out when the battle hymn of the abortion republic is sung? Seeking responses to those questions from those involved in campaigning for 'abortion rights', I have come up against a strange wall of silence, an apparent inability to hear what is to me simply heartfelt, human and authentic. The pro-choice ideology seems chillingly incapable of addressing my pain and the pain of other grieving mothers. It also seems to advance the idea that abortion somehow *in itself* emancipates women. How many modern feminists know about the early feminists who abhorred and condemned abortion, seeing it as an example of men's exploitation and degradation of women? I read the literature of pro-choice hardliners and I wonder why women are making themselves so hard, so brutal, why they seem proud of their lack of feeling or sorrow at abortion, and why they need to mock or deny the suffering of others. Some seem to become so intoxicated with the language of choice, as many ideologues become drunk on the heady wine of noble phrases, that they no longer have minds clear enough to hear the raw and simple reality of what one person is saying to another of her own experience. Chalker and Downes[4] quote an abortion provider in Pennsylvania: 'Women who are against abortion often say that they regret their decision to have one, and many claim they were pressured into it by husbands, boyfriends, or parents, or complain that counselors did not provide them with enough information'. There it is: women's statements about pressure from others or inadequate counselling must be just so much self-serving pretence, and whatever happens abortion must never, never be blamed - only the women who 'claim' they have suffered from it, apparently under the influence of some dubious or hysterical ideological viewpoint. This sort of thing is as offensive, and shallow, as any pro-life literature I have read.

The competing ideologies have another dimension for women who do suffer, or who know that they suffer after abortion: their grief and disturbance are denied or dismissed by those who have a vested interest in doing so. I have heard many first-hand testimonies of women's psychological and emotional distress after abortion being misdiagnosed or ignored by doctors and my own experience bears that out. When the nature of the symptoms that I was experiencing, which I knew clearly were connected to abortion, began to be oppressive and overwhelming, I went to my GP. It is a group practice and over a period I saw several of the doctors in it; attempting to explain the nature of my distress, I met with what seemed like blank incomprehension from all of them. Depression was diagnosed and the usual course of anti-depressants prescribed; eventually I stopped talking about the nightmares, the lack of ability to respond normally and naturally to people (there was an overriding—and unrealistic—desire to withdraw from everyone and live alone in some isolated rural retreat) and the sense of being quite numb and blank, like one half-dead, which was interspersed with moments of intense and almost unbearable sadness.

Eventually I discovered that many of the symptoms I was suffering were those of what is now known as post-traumatic stress disorder, originally observed in US soldiers returning from Vietnam. (The human organism responds to unnatural and overwhelming trauma by erecting a barrier that prevents all feeling; this blocks out the terrible distress at the trauma, but also all positive emotions, so that sufferers complain of being unable to feel, to love, to laugh.) The post-abortion variety of this syndrome has been derided by the pro-choice lobby but all I can say in response is, again, that I experienced it before I heard about it. There are probably many conditions and syndromes that are improperly understood, but why is post-abortion reaction often so singularly misunderstood? Could it partly be because doctors – whose primary duty is to do no harm to their patients (indeed, Hippocrates' oath included a commitment not to abort women) – who regularly refer women for abortion cannot square this with an acknowledgement that at least some of those patients will be severely damaged by the 'treatment' they have sanctioned?

Those who champion abortion as a woman's right to choose naturally do not want to acknowledge that some women wish they had never had such a right in the first place (by the same token, of course, those who see abortion as wrong in all circumstances may discredit women who say they are grateful for having had easy access to legal abortion). Those who supported or encouraged the woman's decision to abort can also refuse to acknowledge her subsequent pain because they themselves, consciously or unconsciously, feel themselves implicated. To accept her suffering would be a tacit admission of guilt at not having offered the right kind of support and encouragement when it was needed. And then the woman herself propagates the secrecy that surrounds abortion by being unable to admit to it. The shame that one feels, compounded by the implicit avowal that one's life was so out of control that one agreed to something that one neither understood nor truly wanted, is probably the most powerful silencer of all.

On the other side of the fence, those who oppose abortion can demonize the woman, treating her as though she were a criminal or at least morally defective, for doing something that is legal and often encouraged. They can seem self-righteously insensitive to the complexity and ambiguity of the situation that led to abortion. By legalizing abortion, society is in effect saying that it is an acceptable solution to an 'unwanted' pregnancy; it can therefore seem like the responsible and necessary thing to do. Even more than that, not having an abortion in difficult circumstances is often presented as the *immoral* option. A woman's guilt at abortion is often terrible, and I have tried to outline my own – but talk of 'murder' is unhelpful, sounds cheap and emotive. It also serves to isolate the woman yet further by throwing the responsibility onto her alone, which is, of course, just what arguments about a woman's right to choose do.

Just as the damage to women is generally so ill-understood, the damage that abortion can cause to a woman's relationship with surviving children and her partner is largely ignored (men can of course suffer on their own account after abortion). Such extended damage is no fanciful notion dreamed up by pro-life campaigners in a bid to undermine the availability of abortion, although it may be so used. I have heard first-hand testimonies from women of an inability to bond with, detachment from or even hostility to subsequent children after an abortion – or of an anxious over-protectiveness that stifles the child and prevents her or him from developing normally. In this sense, abortion can be a time-bomb. It is significantly different to other surgical procedures; when a diseased appendix, for example, is removed, full healing of the body normally ensues, but while a woman's body may return to health after a foetus is removed (though not always, since, from the available evidence, there is an increased risk of breast cancer and of infertility or problems with subsequent pregnancies), permanent damage can be done to her mind and to her spirit. An abortion, rather than healing the 'disease' of pregnancy, can be just the beginning of an affliction whose symptoms ripple outwards. I believe that it is fairly well documented that relationships are more likely to split than survive the death of a child in any circumstances; abortion is no exception and carries with it, of course, the added potential for blame and recrimination. The birth of a child is by no means guaranteed to cement a relationship that is already fragile – however, it seems to me that when life is allowed to take its course, events tend to flow in one's direction, whereas the outcome of violence and destruction tends to be suffering and disharmony. That, once again, is simply the fruit of my observation and experience.

According to the pro-choice camp, most women respond positively and well to abortion; according to the pro-life camp, most suffer the damage and regret that I have suffered. What is the truth? Even if one could establish the exact percentages (an almost impossible task in any case, given the well-established stage of 'denial'; one woman I knew, who has gone through a profound reaction to her abortion, lived for 18 years in the belief that it had not affected her at all), could it touch or alter the fundamental ethical question about the taking of human life? If something is wrong, presumably it remains wrong even if one suffers no adverse effects from it. And even this apparent lack of suffering is problematic, since usually (unless we are psychopathic) we do suffer remorse at what we feel to be wrong and can be experienced as abhorrent by the unconscious, even though the conscious mind may not. In the general fog of denial and ignorance about the effects of abortion on women, the root cause of various physical and psychological symptoms might never be sought and so never located.

The real point, however, is that society has decided that abortion is legal and, deny it or not, for most of us that means that it is also morally permissible. It is sophistry to argue that it is an area in which the state merely declares itself neutral, allowing personal morality to be the arbiter. We do not say that about stealing, we do not say it about child abuse. We do not even say it about cruelty to animals. If I was being asked to separate myself entirely from my society, disregard its mores and drag myself free of its influence – declare myself an independent territory – then I say that I, and most other people, are incapable of doing that. Abortion was not just my decision, it was my society's. Some or most feminists may deride my feeling that I needed protection and support when I was pregnant, not the right to choose the death of my unborn baby. I myself find it hard to admit. Yet I think it is the truth.

So these are my obstinate questionings, the thoughts that have tumbled about in my head over the past years. Rather like contemplating what lies beyond the limits of the universe, trying to weigh life and death in the balance leads to ultimately useless and mind-boggling intellectual speculation – all I can do is ask such questions, or rather watch them tear themselves out of me. Society gave me the right to answer them for myself, but I was not and am not capable of doing so. The few things of which I am certain are emotional and my ethical understanding of abortion arises out of those truths of the heart. What if I had not felt love for my child, what if I had not experienced the wonder of her creation, what if I has simply viewed it as a pregnancy that was inconvenient and that had to be 'got rid of'? What if I had sincerely believed I was doing nothing wrong by having an abortion and had experienced no effects from it rather than relief and gratitude? It is, once more, impossible for me to answer such questions. But even if those were my reactions, it still would not dispense with the fact that I and others had decided to end a human life. Even if I chose not to describe that as an ethical problem, it would not cease to be one.

There has been too much shouting of answers in this debate – and a slogan is nothing if not a bludgeoning answer – and not nearly enough simple, human enquiry. Abortion is offered and performed as though it were an event of little significance and that simplistic and what I would call soulless attitude is the root of the problem. The legalization of abortion has debased it: it is no longer seen for what it is and certain simple, human truths have been obscured by all the ideological (and essentially unreal) barracking. It seems there is no room for the poet's eye or heart in the 'abortion debate', or for the writer's detached, observing gaze. We have collectively passed too utterly, just as I personally have done, from innocence to experience and can no longer admit Blake's insight that true clarity of vision is:

> To see a world in a grain of sand,
> And heaven in a wild flower
> Hold infinity in the palm of your hand,
> And eternity in an hour.

It is also this phenomenon that the old Jewish proverb describes: 'He who saves a single life is as if he saved the entire universe.' I know the truth of that, not as an item of dogma in some dreary religious or ideological programme, but in my guts, in my being. I do not place any form of knowledge higher.

As I was writing these concluding lines, a letter arrived from the friend who had earlier written telling me about the abortion that had been so right for her.

In it, she told me that her mother was dying of cancer and that things had taken on a different perspective; she now felt that there was no great divide between us, which I understood to mean that she accepted my sad feelings, and perhaps her own, about abortion. She wanted to see me, to talk. This small *deux ex machina* might seem rather too neat, a device I felt justified in cooking up in the interests of a fitting finale, but it really did happen: perhaps one could just say that it was the power of life – and the power of life in death – exerting its ineluctable hold, even over late twentieth-century western civilization.

NOTES

1 I do not know the gender of my child but it helps the grieving process if one is assigned and a name given.
2 Sereny, G., *Albert Speer: His Battle with Truth* (Macmillan, London, 1995).
3 Chalker, R. and Downes, C., *A Woman's Book of Choices: Abortion, Menstrual Extraction, RU486* (Four Walls Eight Windows, New York, 1992).
4 Ibid.
5 William Blake, 'Auguries of Innocence'.

Conclusion

ANGELA KENNEDY

FEMINISM AND SLIPPERY SLOPES

There are many other voices, besides those of feminists, in the abortion debate. As abortion is considered a life and death issue by many, it becomes related to other life and death issues. Abortion proponents, not necessarily feminist at all, often frame their arguments as part of a consistent advocacy of what Wolf Wolfensburger has termed 'death-making decisions'.[1]

One such utilitarian philosopher, for example, Peter Singer, advocates infanticide for disabled babies, or indeed any baby that society deems unfit.[2] Infanticide of females has a long tradition and is still practised today (together with foeticide),[3] and present day apologists for the practice express unchallenged assumptions that can only be described as sexist (except here, we are referring to children actually losing their lives because they are female). Singer and co-author Helena Kuhse inform us of, for example, the 'necessity' of killing baby girls among the Netsilik Eskimos because of the reliance 'on adult males' for survival, that is, because males hunted for meat, even while women 'gathered plant food during the summer'.[4] Singer's analysis appears to come from a standpoint in which male skills are valued more than female skills, and in which meat is valued more than vegetation as food, even though, universally, hunting for meat is often an unsuccessful exercise, and the plant food gathered by females is often what sustains communities.[5] Reay Tannahill states that infanticide was a common and 'obvious' way of population control, and believes that:

> It was probably the female child who was the victim, *not for male chauvinist reasons* [my italics] but because she herself was a child producer of the future, a threat not only in her person but in her progeny to the food supply . . . .[6]

Tannahill's own functionalist approval of various gynocidal practices is shown by her contemptuous assertion that 'It was self-indulgent humanitarianism that led the British to suppress practices such as sati [*sic*] (funeral pyre leaping) and female infanticide . . .'[7]

Singer and Kuhse also attempt to persuade us that infanticide is often practised freely and willingly by women.[8] This brings us to a most worrying aspect: some of the apologists for infanticide are feminist. Penelope Brown advances a 'general' feminist view that:

... to control childbirth via abortion, or contraception or infanticide are ...
important aspects of women's status.[9]

Here, Brown appears to be assuming that infanticide is a valid means of women
exercising control over their own fertility. Germaine Greer sees infanticide as a
less dangerous option of fertility control than abortion (for the woman rather
than the child, of course).[10]

I have discussed infanticide at length because certain utilitarian philosophers
who do advocate the practice are able to do so because abortion advocacy has
become such an entrenched notion in modern western society. Pro-abortion
feminist doctrine has been at least partly responsible for this slippery slope in
moral reasoning. Because the distinction between foetuses and infants are
arbitrary and becoming more blurred (particularly with medical advances), and
because pro-abortion feminists have been so determined to promote abortion, it
is becoming more and more difficult for very young human beings to be assigned
the protective status of 'personhood'. As we have seen, the sub-groups even more
likely to be unprotected are very young female humans, as well as babies with
disabilities.

It is also very important that we consider the functionalist arguments for
abortion, such as those professed by de Beauvoir,[11] or Germaine Greer,[12] in the
same context as Singer's arguments for infanticide. They all express an implicit
approval of cultural organization, in which women are expected to internalize
oppression and perpetuate practices 'for the good of the others', whether
individual men, or cultures as a whole. The psychological bonds that women
might feel for their children, born or unborn, are completely disregarded in most
of these narratives. Abortion and infanticide are closely linked to other practices
of mutilation or coercion of women, such as footbinding, female circumcision,
suttee, and even modern day cosmetic surgery. Jane Ussher, for example, links
female circumcision, a cultural practice, with cosmetic surgery. She acknowledges that 'To say that women are responsible for this process is facile (and of
course misogynist)'.[13] It is easily argued that, for pro-life feminists, in acknowledging abortion or infanticide as oppressive acts (for both women and children),
the practices must be considered within their cultural contexts, and therefore
labelling women as 'responsible' for their own oppression is completely inappropriate. It is especially so when done by advocates of these oppressive practices.

The difficulties in reconciling concern for women's rights and human rights
with abortion advocacy has become conspicuous by the absence of public
feminist deliberation on some recent issues in reproductive and abortion technology, such as the 'harvesting' of female foetal ova,[14] embryo destruction, and
a new method of termination, 'partial birth abortion', in which the foetus/baby
is allowed to pass through the vaginal canal until only the head remains inside
the mother's body, and then the skull is pierced and the brain aspirated,
collapsing the skull in the process.[15] From my own standpoint, I was horrified

and sickened even in writing this description of the procedure, and have looked in vain for a similar response from pro-choice feminists. I do not believe my own and others' feelings of revulsion are misplaced. I would, for example, also expect other feminists to be appalled at infanticide. The apparent disparity of reactions to images of violence between feminists points to a possible collective denial by pro-choice feminists, both of women's experiences that do not fit in with the pro-choice worldview, and of the psychological reactions of pro-choice feminists themselves. Feminists are finding themselves left behind in the public debates about reproductive technology and other life and death issues, because a consistent advocacy of abortion is seen as the authoritative feminist viewpoint alone, and the problems of that viewpoint have not been seriously considered enough by feminism; yet.

GETTING BACK TO STANDPOINTS

There are a number of pro-life feminist standpoints that we have not been able to include as first-person narratives in this work. The standpoints of some pro-life women of religious faiths have been expressed in other works.[16] While some of the contributors may have a religious faith of their own, their arguments against abortion are consistent with secular arguments, including those made by contributors who are not religious. The first-person views of Third World women and women of other ethnic groups have not been included, purely because at this stage in pro-life feminist discourse in Europe, at least, it has been very difficult to find such women who feel able to express such views, despite much endeavour on the part of the editor to give space to those standpoints. There may be specific reasons for this. One possible explanation, that might be offered by pro-choice feminists, cynical of the standpoints expressed in this book, would be that there are no such women. But even the few narratives that we have already referred to point to the existence of such women. Other, more likely explanations, are that Third World women, and women of colour, do not yet have a firm enough standing in western feminist discourse for any such views to be expressed. Indeed, Caroline Ramazanoglu has pointed to the need for feminists to find new ways of making connections which avoid the 'power relationship of the "helper/helped dyad" that has characterized white women's relations with black women'.[17] Bobbi Sykes, a Black Australian woman quoted by Ramazanoglu, gives a chilling example of some white feminist reaction to those who object to abortion in any way:

> A male interviewer organized a prominent white movement woman to debate the subject with me on television. Unfortunately, the woman used the opportunity to scream at me that I wasn't the right sort of black, and that I didn't have a dozen children and live in the creek-bed at Alice Springs . . . That I,

representing an opinion of the Black community, brazenly dared to confront and oppose an option of the white community, was sufficient to crack the veneer over the movement woman's racism, and through that crack spewed forth the most virulent and racist comments that I had heard publicly for some time . . . Privately, many similar events occur constantly.[18]

If Third World women and women of other ethnic groups are still struggling to break free of white western feminist domination, even as they struggle against racial oppression and male domination, then perhaps it is not surprising that there might still be some reluctance on the part of individual women to publicly make any objections to abortion. It has also been very difficult to find lesbians or disabled women willing to reveal a pro-life feminist standpoint in the first person, possibly for very similar reasons (although there are some disabled women who criticize certain aspects of abortion when specifically related to pre-natal screening for disability, for example).[19]

But feminism needs their standpoints. The potential of feminism to transform society has hardly been realized. Improvements in the relations between women and men, as well as many other dynamics within humanity, still need to be made. But Ramazanoglu has shown that the huge diversity of feminist activity globally has drawn increasing differences between women, and:

It is only if these differences can be identified, clarified, and dealt with that effective strategies for the liberation of women can be clearly worked out.[20]

Abortion has proved to be one of those issues capable of dividing women. Elizabeth Fox-Genovese has described abortion as 'the central issue that divides them [women], and as the central metaphor for the nature of our society'.[21] It is therefore necessary for feminists to make an urgent priority of working out differences and resolving them in ways that do not devalue the standpoint of some women. Unfortunately, up to now, many pro-choice feminist descriptions of pro-life women's standpoints, made in the third person, have done just that, as each commentator, from her position of power which the published written word gives her, hazards descriptions of pro-life women's beliefs, and then denigrates them. This has been achieved, for example, by such writers as Andrea Dworkin,[22] Ellen Willis, Deirdre English[23] and Kristin Luker.[24] In fact, Laurie Shage describes Luker's work as such:

Luker seems to be interested in exposing the cultural presuppositions of 'pro-life women' in order to show that they are really not concerned to protect life so much as to protect traditional gender roles for women. In doing this, Luker may be encouraging us to discount the belief systems of 'pro-life' women, and to see them as self-deceived. That is, in some parts of her book, Luker appears to be uncovering the cultural assumptions of 'pro-life' women through the distorting lenses of 'pro-choice' women. Because she does not attempt the reverse, I see her as ultimately striving for the total victory of one side in this debate.[25]

However, the relatively recent and growing practice of publicly submitting their own standpoints for scrutiny among feminist commentators, as well as the scrutinizing by feminists of standpoints, is contributing to a fuller understanding of many important issues for feminism, including abortion.

FEMINISM COMES OF AGE?

In 1984, a North American collaborative project between pro-life and pro-choice women (and one man) sought to 'illuminate, enrich, and deepen the dialogue on abortion'.[26] Wife and husband partnership Sidney and Daniel Callaghan (Sidney is 'pro-life', while Daniel is 'pro-choice') brought together a wide range of views, including those of Sandra Harding and Jean Bethke Elshtain. In true adherence to 'standpoint' principles, each contributor had to submit a short autobiography for scrutiny. The theme of the book is devoted to understanding and respecting differences, and searching for ways to effect dialogue and useful compromises. The differences are not hidden, and occasional flashes of antagonism surface. Yet the bringing together of diverse views in such a way must itself be considered a great achievement, considering the hostility that is usually engendered in any debate about abortion. Importantly, what is shown by the volume is the inadequacy of the labels often ascribed to those who take part in the abortion debate, as well as the 'complicated continuum of positions' that stretch from a total rejection to a total support for abortion.[27]

As has been shown, British and Irish 'mainstream' feminism has yet to achieve such insight into the abortion issue, though occasional pockets of co-operation happen. The Women's Coalition, for example, is a newly founded political party of women in Northern Ireland with the aim of 'rupturing the traditional unionist-republican debate and counteracting the invisibility of women in Northern Irish party politics'. Their collective aspirations mean that as an organization, they are able to reconcile the containment of many different backgrounds, including 'left and right, green and orange, anti-abortion and pro-choice, rural and urban backgrounds'.[28] They are unequivocally opposed to violence.

Such insight is needed on a larger scale if feminism is to remain a consistent and successful force for advancing parity for women,[29] as the parity of women cannot be achieved unless parity for all is achieved. Feminism may have to consider the rights of unborn children, if we are to demand continued consideration for the rights of women. And there are ways in which compromise between pro-life feminists and pro-choice feminists can be reached; a commitment to giving all women contemplating abortion the opportunity to make a fully informed decision, for example, the promotion of viable alternatives to abortion wherever possible, a concerted effort to ensure that reproductive choice means ensuring women are not forced into abortion, campaigning for support for women in crisis pregnancies, and more collaborative works in which dialogue about abortion can be engaged. Elizabeth Fox–Genovese describes the necessity of this succinctly:

> Abortion, perhaps more than any other issue, demonstrates how much we need a collective discourse of problem solving, a practical ethic . . . Above all, we need a recognition that we have no rights independent of responsibilities, except perhaps the right to insist that society recognize its obligation to permit us to meet our responsibiliites. Yes, abortion commands our rethinking, if only because the very existence of abortion as an issue betokens what we, as women, inescapably share.[30]

NOTES

1 Wolfensburger, W., *The New Genocide of Handicapped and Afflicted People* (Syracuse University Training Institute, New York, 1992).
2 Singer, P. and Kuhse, H., *Should the Baby Live? The Problem of Handicapped Infants* (Oxford University Press, Oxford, 1985)
3 Venkatram, S., 'Girl Infanticide Rife in India', *Nursing Standard*, 6 September 1995.
4 Singer and Kuhse, op. cit., 99–100.
5   See, for example, Adams, C., *The Sexual Politics of Meat* (Polity Press, London, 1992).
6 Tannahill, R., *Sex in History* (Hamish Hamilton, London, 1980), 31–2.
7 Op cit., 315.
8 Singer and Kuhse, 100–9.
9 Brown, P., 'Universals and Particulars', Cambridge Women's Studies Group (eds.), *Women in Society: Interdisciplinary Essays* (Virago, London, 1981), 251.
10 Greer, G., *Sex and Destiny* (Picador, London,1984), 188.
11 See Introduction.
12 Greer, op. cit., 188–93.
13   Ussher, J. M., *The Psychology of the Female Body* (Routledge, London, 1989), 33–4.
14 Kennedy, A., 'Great Britain's Debate over the Utilization of Fetal Ova', *Studies in Prolife Feminism*, vol. 1, no. 3, Summer 1995, 191–201.
15 See Appleyard, B., 'Abortion: Why We Must Think Again', *The Independent*, 18 July 1996.
16 For example, see Tickle, P. (ed.), *Confessing Conscience: Churched Women on Abortion* (Abingdon Press, Nashville, 1990).
17 Ramazanoglu, C., *Feminism and the Contradictions of Oppression* (Routledge, London, 1989), 191, quoting Sykes, B. in Rowland, R., *Women Who Do and Women Who Don't Join the Women's Movement* (Routledge & Kegan Paul, London, 1984), 64.
18 Sykes, B., op. cit., 65.
19 See Chapter 6.
20 Ramazanoglu, op. cit., vii.
21 Fox Genovese, E., 'Rethinking Abortion in Terms of Human Interconnectedness', *Studies in Prolife Feminism*, vol. 1 no. 2, Spring, 1995, 103.
22 Dworkin, A., *Right–Wing Women: The Politics of Domesticated Females* (Women's Press, London, 1988).
23 See Willis, E., 'Feminism, Moralism and Pornography', English, D., 'The Fear That Feminism

Will Free Men First', and Willis, E., 'Abortion: Is a Woman a Person?' in Snitow, A. Stansell, C. Thompson, S. (eds.), *Powers of Desire: The Politics of Sexuality* (New Feminist Library, New York, 1993), for examples of this.

24 Luker, K., *Abortion and the Politics of Motherhood* (University of California Press, Berkeley, 1984).

25 Shage, L., *Moral Dilemmas of Feminism* (Routledge, London, 1994), 194.

26 Callaghan, S. and Callaghan, D., *Abortion: Understanding Differences* (Plenum Press, New York, 1984), xvi.

27 Meehan, M., 'More Trouble than They're Worth? Children and Abortion', in Callaghan and Callaghan, 178.

28 Wynne-Jones, R., 'Irish Talks: Men Posture, Women Progress', *The Independent on Sunday*, 16 June 1996.

29 See Ellis, C., 'Equality Will Not Make Us Equal' *New Statesman and Society*, 1 November 1991. Cynthia Cockburn states that we should be aiming, not for equality for women inserted one by one into the unresponsive framework of mankind, but for *parity* between the two sexes, separately specified as comprising humankind. The concept of such a parity, or equivalence, has been introduced within the context of the European Community, a *democratie paritaire*.

30 Fox Genovese, op. cit., 103.

Notes on Contributors

ANGELA KENNEDY was born in 1963. She is a writer with a background in Health and Safety and Nursing, who contributes to various publications including socialist, feminist, nursing, and health and safety journals. She has two children. She has compiled an anthology of short stories and has contributed to other short story anthologies. An active peace campaigner as a young woman, she is now Women's Officer of the Labour Life Group. She is currently engaged in a Master's Degree in Gender Studies at Middlesex University.

MARY KRANE DERR is a poet, non-fiction writer, and social service professional. Her belief in complete non-violence has been shaped by her experience as a woman with multiple disabilities; healing from childhood abuse; bearing and rearing an unplanned child, caring for animals and studying biology; and engaging in interreligious dialogue. With this anthology, she is going back to her roots in more than one sense. She is a European American whose family tree includes refugees from the Irish potato famine, one of the first Congregational ministers in England, and a woman accused at the Salem Witch trials. She lives in Chicago with her husband, young daughter, and, whenever possible, sentient beings of other species. She is co-editor of *Pro-life Feminism: Yesterday and Today*, published in the US by Sulzburger & Graham, New York, 1995.

BREDA O'BRIEN is a founder member of the group Feminists for Life of Ireland. Formerly working in Television, she now teaches in a comprehensive school, and is a full-time mother to Ben, born in September 1993. She is actively involved in women's rights and human rights campaigns in Ireland. She lives in Dublin.

DIANA FORREST has two degrees, a BSc in Mathematic and a BA honours in English. She was editor of the quarterly journal of the group Feminists against Eugenics from 1989–1992. She is active in pro-life, peace and other radical movements. She was involved in the British Withdrawal from Northern Ireland Campaign and was an early member of the group Women for Life. She helped revive the Women's Co-Operative Guild White Poppy campaign, first distributing white poppies for Remembrance day, 1976. She was formerly a member of the 'Survivors' pro-life street theatre group. She lives in Todmorden, near Yorkshire.

ANN FARMER is Chair of the Labour Life Group, a pro-life group within the Labour Party. She is editor of their magazine *Labour Life Group News*. She is a member of the Labour Party and CND and ALERT. She is a freelance writer, poet, journalist and cartoonist. Her published work includes articles on mental health, and on family life. She is the author of *The Language of Life*, published by St Paul's Press. She works on justice and peace initiatives within her Parish in Woodford Green, Essex. She has three children.

ALI BROWNING obtained her BA in Peace Studies at Bradford University, where she contributed to the student magazine on peace and feminist issues. She is a human and animal rights campaigner and is particularly concerned with the rights of poor and single women, and with the rights of children. She is involved with the Middle Eastern Peace movement in Yorkshire, where she lives. She writes fiction, particularly children's stories, and non-fiction articles for a number of journals and newspapers.

MARIE-CLAIRE DARKE has been married to a man with Spina Bifida and Hydrocephalus – the 'congenital' – for thirteen years. She has a young son and obtained her degree in Spanish at the University of Wolverhampton, after migrating from the medical profession in Surrey. Aged 37, she is currently working towards a postgraduate qualification in social work.

RACHEL MACNAIR graduated with honours from Earlham College, with a major in Peace and Conflict Studies. She has been active in the peace movement since campaigning against the Vietnam war from the age of 14. Rachel was President of Feminists For Life of America from 1984–1994. She is the founder of the Susan B. Anthony List, which raises money for pro-life women candidates to run for public office. Rachel is currently Vice-President of the Seamless Garment Network and Editor-in-Chief of the international journal *Studies in Pro-life Feminism*, produced by the Feminism and Nonviolence Studies Association. She is co-editor of *Pro-life Feminism: Yesterday and Today*, and a forthcoming book on the psychological effects of performing abortions.

PATRICIA CASEY qualified as a doctor in 1976 from University College Cork. She studied post-graduate psychiatry in Britain, working in both clinical practice and research. In 1991 she became the first woman Professor of Psychiatry at Uuniversity College Dublin and the Mater Misericordiae Hospital. She has written *A Guide to Psychiatry in Primary Care* and *Social Function: The Hidden Axis of Classification*, and has contributed to 15 academic texts and written on 60 research papers, as well as frequent broadcasts and media articles. She is chair of the Fitness to Practice Committee for the Medical Council. She is married with two adopted children.

CATHERINE SPENCER read English at the University of Wales before going to work in France as a teacher and a freelance journalist. She then lived and worked in India as a research assistant and translator. She translates fiction and non-fiction from French into English and has worked since 1989 as an editor of *Hansard* at the House of Commons.

Index

abolitionists, 20, 21
abortifacients 41
abortion
  illegal 49, 77
  legalization of 43, 48, 53, 63, 77
  methods of 6–7,
  negligence and 111–112
  practice of 76, 77, 78–79, 110
  side effects of 36, 79, 80–81, 95
  as 'technical fix' 36, 44
  and violence 82
Abortion Act 1967 50, 51
Abortion Information Act 1995 88
abortionists 76, 77, 81–82
adoption 86–89
Anderson, Elizabeth Garrett 15
animals 57, 59, 62, 64
Angelou, Maya 8
Anna O. 22
antibiotics, effect on contraceptive pill 76
Anthony, Susan B. 17, 21
antifeminism 2
Appleton, Joan 80–81
Aristotle 67

Barry, Kathleen 31, 32
de Beauvoir, Simone 3, 30, 110
Benda 30
Bensing, Sandra 75
birth control see contraception
Blackwell, Elizabeth 15, 17, 18, 19
black women 5, 70, 111–112
breast cancer 79
Breuer, Josef 22
Brinkerhoff, Mattie 12
Brown, Penelope 109
Browne, Stella 22

Callaghan, Sidney and Daniel 113
capitalism 43–44, 46, 48
Catholicism 6
child abuse 50, 82
Child Support Agency 39
China 67

choice 35, 36, 43, 49, 53–54, 75
  of abortion 33, 34
  as ideology 33
Claflin, Tennesee 16
consciousness raising 78
Corrigan, Mairead 8
contraceptive pill 39
contraception 19, 41, 42, 53, 58
cosmetic surgery 110
Currie, Edwina 54

Dahlrup, Drude 48
Davis, Paulina Wright 19
death penalty 8
Delmar, Rosalind 28
democratie paritaire 115
Denfield, Rene 4
disabled people 64, 68, 69, 70, 112
divorce 40
Doe v. Bolton 75
Douglas, Mary 68
Duffey, Eliza Bisbee 19, 20
Duster, Troy 69
Dworkin, Andrea 112

economics 42, 43, 44, 45, 71–72
Eisenstein, Hester 2
embryo, research on 36
Emily's List 56
employment 42
English, Deirdre 112
equality 43, 44, 47, 50, 51, 83, 113–114
equal pay 39
Equal Opportunities Commission 43
eugenics 8, 67, 90
euthanasia 8, 53, 64
Evans, Elizabeth Edson 21
Everywoman 62

families 44–45
female circumcision 110
feminism 1–11, 28, 47, 54
  and abortion 28, 29, 54
  types of 2

and infanticide 110–111
  and life or death issues 111
  and reproductive technology debates 111
Feminists Against Eugenics 7
Feminists for Life of America 7, 14
Feminists for Life of Ireland 7
Fetrow, Judith 82
foeticide 36
foetus 44
  interpretations of 30, 31, 61–64
  development 20, 32, 36, 59–61, 79, 83, 90
  disabled 50, 63, 64, 69, 72, 73, 92–94
  pain 60–61, 65
  sentience 64
footbinding 110
Foucault, Michel 73
Fox-Genovese, Elizabeth 112
Freely, Maureen 3, 36
Freire, Paolo 29, 30
French, Dr Anna Densmore 20
Freud, Sigmund 22
Fuller, Caroline 17
Fund for the Feminist Majority 14

Gage, Matilda Joslyn 17, 20
genetic counselling 69
Gilligan, Carol 32
Goltz, Pat 23
Gordon, Linda 16
Gorman, Teresa 54
Greer, Germaine 1, 110

Hamer, Fannie Lou 24–25
Harding, Sandra 1, 4, 6, 113
Hayat, Abu 76, 77
Hooker, Isabella Beecher 16, 19
housing 39, 40
Human Fertilisation and Embryology Act 1990 67

illegitimacy 86–87
incest 83

infanticide,
  of female infants 67 109
  of disabled infants 67, 109
  advocacy of 109, 110, 111
  and hunter/gatherer cultures
    109
  in vitro fertilization 4

Jeffreys, Sheila 43
Judge, Evelyn 23
Judischer Frauenbund 23

Kirk, Eleanor 17, 21
Klein, Renate 36
Koop, Everett 81
Kuhse, Helena 109

Labour Life Group 8
Labour Party 47, 50, 52
lesbians 1, 40, 112
Lozier, Charlotte Denman 17–18
Luker, Kristin 112–113

McWhinnie, Dr Alexina 88
Madame Restell 15, 17
Madonna 54
Mackinnon, Catherine 4
Malthusianism 52
marriage 41
Matthewes Green, Frederica 76
McCorvey, Norma 75
medical profession 4
menopause 83
menstruation 83
Miles, Rosalind 88
Mill, John Stuart 16
Miller, Alice 80
miscarriage 35, 58, 82
Moran, Andrew 18
Morris, Jenny 63, 74
Mother Teresa 54
motherhood 36, 48
  'voluntary' 19
  'enforced' 19

National Abortion Campaign 50
National Abortion Federation 77
Nazis 73
Neuberger, Rabbi Julia 86
Neustatter, Angela 3
Newlife group 8
New Right 1, 8, 9
Nilson, Lennart 32

Norton, Sarah F. 21
Northern Ireland 50, 113

Oakley, Anne 5
Olivarez, Graciela 24
'overpopulation' 51

Paglia, Camille 2
Pankhurst, Sylvia 22
Pappenheim, Bertha 22–23
Parliament 39, 50, 51
patriarchy 2, 29, 38, 41, 73
Paul, Alice 23
'permissiveness' 40, 41, 42
Pitts Hames, Margie 75
PLAGAL (Pro-life Alliance of Gays
  and Lesbians) 8
pornography 1, 2, 33, 38, 40, 42, 43
Post-abortion Syndrome 81, 105
Poverty 39, 40, 46, 49
pregnancy 83, 94–95
  crisis 22, 24, 36, 41, 53, 114
pre-natal testing 68, 92
prostitution 19, 22, 23, 33, 38,
  40, 42, 43, 48

'quality of life' arguments 53, 68,
  69, 70, 93

racism 112
Radcliffe-Richards, Janet 91
Ramazanoglu, Caroline 111, 112
rape 14, 35, 40, 42, 76, 83, 90–92
Rapport d'Uriel 30
religion 57, 58
reproductive technology 4, 110
Revolution, The 17
Rhonnda's (Lady) Six Point Group 22
Rich, Adrienne 36
'right-to-life' 33, 89
Roe v. Wade 24, 75
Rowbothan, Sheila 22
Rowlands, Robin 2
Russia 48
Ruzek, Sheryl 28
RU486 52

Saunders, Lesley 33, 34, 35
Savage, Wendy 63
Schneiders, Sandra 28, 29
Seamless Garment Network 8
sex 38, 40, 41, 42, 45
  'child-free' 41, 42

Shulman, Alix Kates 2
Silent Scream, The 62
Singer, Peter 65, 66, 109, 110
single mothers 49
Smith, Laura Cuppy 21
socialism 47, 49
socialist attitudes to anti-abortion-
  ists 48, 54, 55
Specific Issue Anatagonists 3
Spender, Dale 12, 14
standpoints 4–7, 111–113
Stanton, Elizabeth Cady v, 14, 16,
  17, 20
Steinberg, Deborah Lynn 4
Steinem, Gloria 4
Stockham, Dr Alice Bunker 18, 20
Stopes, Marie 52
suicide 94–95
surrogacy 36
Sykes, Bobbi 111–112

Tannahill, Reay 109
thalidomide 51
Thatcher, Margaret 53
Third World women 111, 112
Tisdale, Sallie 78
tokology 19
Tolstoy, Leo 19
Tribe, Laurence 29

ultrasound 78
Uri, Constance Redbird 23–24
Ussher, Jane 110

Vaughan, Hester 21
vivisection 5

*Webster v. Reproductive Health
  Services* 15–16
welfare state 48, 49
Willard, Frances 21
Willis, Ellen 112
Women for Life 8
Wolf, Naomi 3, 35
Wolfensburger, Wolf 109
Wollstonecraft, Mary 13, 18
womb, woman as 38, 39
Woman's Coalition, the 113
Woodhull, Victoria 16, 18, 19, 20,
  21
Wright, Henry Clarke 21

'X', Ms 94